CHARACTER CALISTHENICS

by Coach Elliot Johnson

Illustrated by Jerry Byrd

PRESS

Library of Congress Control Number: 2002113855
ISBN 1-591603-93-5

For information concerning additional materials write:

WINNING RUN FOUNDATION
One University Avenue
Bourbonnais, IL 60914

Table of Contents

Table of Contents (Continued)

CHARACTER CALISTHENICS
Introduction

WHAT WOULD YOU REQUEST if God appeared to you in a dream and said, "Ask for whatever you want me to give you." That was the question He asked King Solomon many years ago (1 Kings 3:4-12). Do you know what Solomon requested? He humbly asked for a discerning heart to better govern the people and to distinguish between right and wrong. God was so pleased with Solomon's unselfishness, He made him the wisest king who ever lived (v. 12) — and besides that, He gave him riches and honor, too! What a generous Heavenly Father.

In his supernatural wisdom, Solomon wrote 3,000 proverbs and 1,005 songs (1 Kings 4:32). The book of Proverbs contains under 1,000 of his sayings. The Proverbs are short sentences based upon his long experience. All are morally uplifting and easy to remember. All are scientifically accurate, for there are no fables found in God's Word.

All of us need to exercise our bodies to keep them strong and healthy. We do this through stretching and strengthening exercises called calisthenics. We also need calisthenics to stretch and strengthen our character.

The purpose of this book is to strengthen your character. The first step is to get on the Lord's team. Turn to the Appendix on page 144 and make sure you are on the winning team before proceeding.

Each day, make it your plan to examine one character trait. Read the short story, then do the *Character Calisthenics, Short Sprints, Mind Stretchers,* and *Grip Strengtheners* by looking up the verses and answering the questions. You'll need a copy of God's Word — the New International Version. And you must be prepared to search several books of the Bible, for other passages add much to our understanding of character. Definitions of related words are given in the margin. As you do your "Character Calisthenics," may they make you spiritually strong for His glory.

THE PURPOSE of the PROVERBS

"MONEY AND ENDORSMENTS are ruining the game," said Isaiah Thomas of the Detroit Pistons in 1990. Isaiah had just been named MVP of the NBA Finals, but seeing the lack of team purpose as a motivation for playing disturbed him. Because players are paid according to points scored, many play simply for the purpose of statistics and dollars.

"Basketball is not an individual sport. It's a team sport," said Isaiah. "We've been used to dealing with people saying, 'me, me, me.' That's not the way it should be.

"Team basketball — that's the way James Naismith invented it. That's the way it's supposed to be played."

APPLICATION

GOD HAD A HIGH PURPOSE when He inspired Solomon to write the Proverbs. In fact, He had several wonderful purposes. They are listed in Chapter 1, verses 1-6.

DEFINITIONS:

Purpose — "intention, resolve, or plan."

Wisdom — "the ability to see things as God sees them."

Discipline — "self-control, character, orderliness, and efficiency in one's life."

Prudent — "cautious and discreet in conduct, sensible."

Knowledge — "awareness of facts."

CHARACTER CALISTHENICS:

What is the Purpose of the Proverbs?

The proverbs of Solomon son of David, king of Israel: for attaining _____ and _____ ; for _____ words of _____ , for acquiring a _____ and _____ life, doing what is _____ and _____ and _____ ; for giving _____ to the simple, _____ and _____ to the young — let the wise listen and add to their _____ , and let the discerning get _____ — for _____ proverbs and parables, the sayings and riddles of the wise.

Proverbs 1:1-6

What is the Beginning of Knowledge?

The _____ of the _____ is the beginning of knowledge, but _____ despise wisdom and discipline.

Proverbs 1:7

Who is the Wisdom of God?

. . . but to those whom God has called, both Jews and Greeks, _____ the power of God and the _____ of God.

1 Corinthians 1:24

Discretion — "being careful about what one does and says; prudence."

Proverbs — "short sayings of deep truth."

Parable — "a short story to teach a lesson."

Fool — "one who is morally lacking."

SHORT SPRINTS:

1. Paul's purpose was to know Christ (Philippians 3:10).　　T　　F
2. Suffering is related to knowing Christ's power (Philippians 3:10).　　T　　F
3. The final result of Paul's purpose is the resurrection from death (Philippians 3:11).　　T　　F

MIND STRETCHERS:

Who do you know who has definite purpose in life?

Who or what gives him that purpose?

STRENGTHEN YOUR GRIP:

Write out Philippians 3:14:

_____

_____

_____

_____

THE PURPOSE OF PROVERBS AND OF PAUL IS THAT WE MIGHT KNOW CHRIST — THE WISDOM AND POWER OF GOD.

Dear Lord,
Help me to study for the purpose of gaining
the character of Christ.

Amen.

CONFIDENCE

CONNIE MACK was a great baseball manager, having led the Philadelphia Athletics from 1900-1950. Connie once made a great statement on confidence. He said, "I've seen boys on my baseball team go into a slump and never come out of it, and I've seen others snap right out and come back better than ever. I guess more players lick themselves than are ever licked by the opposing team!"

APPLICATION

CONFIDENCE in one's abilities is an essential part of the mindset of a successful athlete. Confidence in the Lord is crucial in our Christian walk. It is important that our confidence in the Lord remains unshaken, even when we go through trying times. The Bible has much to say about the worthiness of God and our trust in Him.

DEFINITIONS:

Acknowledge — "to see God as active in every situation."

Confidence — "trust in."

CHARACTER CALISTHENICS:

Who is our Confidence and What will He Do?

_____ in the _____ with all your _____ and lean not on your own _____ ; in _____ your ways _____ Him, and he will make your _____ straight.

Proverbs 3:5, 6

Have no _____ of sudden _____ or of the _____ that overtakes the _____ , for the Lord will be your _____ and will keep your _____ from being _____ .

Proverbs 3:25, 26

What Are We To Do with Confidence?

Let us then _____ the throne of _____ with _____ , so that we may receive _____ and find _____ to help us in our time of _____ .

Hebrews 4:16

Therefore, brothers, since we have _____
to enter the Most Holy place by the _____
of _____ . . .

Hebrews 10:19

What Will Be the Outcome of Our Confidence?
So do not throw away your _____ ; it
will be richly _____ .

Hebrews 10:35

SHORT SPRINTS:

1. God never forsakes His people (Hebrews 13:5).   T   F
2. The Lord will not help us (Hebrews 13:6).   T   F
3. We should be fearful of life (Hebrews 13:6).   T   F

MIND STRETCHERS:

Who do you know who has extreme confidence?

What is the basis for your confidence?

STRENGTHEN YOUR GRIP:

Write out Hebrews 10:23:

_____

_____

_____

_____

**WE CAN LIVE WITH GREAT CONFIDENCE
BECAUSE OF WHO GOD IS
AND BECAUSE OF WHAT JESUS HAS DONE FOR US.**

Dear Lord,
*   Thank you for your promise to walk beside me*
and to direct my paths.

*   Amen.*

DILIGENCE

TOM SEAVER was one of baseball's best pitchers of all time. He won the Cy Young Award three times. Once, after an exhausting road trip, Tom didn't go straight home from the airport. Because it was his day to throw and he had not done so, he called a cab and went to the darkened stadium where he threw alone for twenty minutes into a screen.

Tom's diligence carried over into the off-season. "If it means in the winter I eat cottage cheese instead of chocolate chip cookies to keep my weight down, then I eat cottage cheese," he said. "I enjoy that cottage cheese more than I would those cookies because it will help me do what makes me happy."

APPLICATION

THE DILIGENCE of Tom Seaver is rare among many people today. But no one reaches his full potential without diligence and self-discipline.

DEFINITIONS:

Diligence — "Constant and careful effort, perseverance."

Sluggard — "A lazy, slothful person."

Fantasies — "Extravagant mental images"

Judgment — "Discernment and common sense."

Poverty — "Lack of food, clothing, and shelter."

Shiftless — "Unable to stick to a task."

CHARACTER CALISTHENICS:

What Example Does the Bible Give of Diligence?

Go to the _____ , you _____ :
consider its ways and be _____ ! It has no
_____ , no _____ , or _____ , yet it
_____ its provisions in _____
and gathers its _____ at _____ .

Proverbs 6:6-8

What are the Results of Diligence and Hard Work?

He who _____ his land will have abundant
_____ , but he who chases _____ lacks
_____ .

Proverbs 12:11

Diligent _____ will _____ ,
but _____ ends in _____ labor.

Proverbs 12:24

All _____ work brings a _____ : but
mere _____ leads only to _____ .

Proverbs 14:23

What Sort of Person is the Opposite of the Diligent?
One who is _____ in his _____ is brother
to one who _____ .

Proverbs 18:9

_____ brings on deep _____ ,
and the _____ man goes _____ .

Proverbs 19:15

The _____ craving will be the _____
of him, because his hands refuse to _____ .

Proverbs 21:25

SHORT SPRINTS:

1. Poverty follows laziness (Proverbs 12:27).   T   F
2. A diligent man prizes his possessions (Proverbs 12:27).   T   F
3. Haste leads to poverty (Proverbs 21:5).   T   F

MIND STRETCHERS:

Who is the most diligent person you know?

Do you know someone who is lazy?

What sort of a person do you want to be?

How can you be more diligent in sports?

At home?

In school?

STRENGTHEN YOUR GRIP:
Write out Proverbs 10:4:

_____

_____

_____

_____

> ### GOD HAS WORDS OF PRAISE
> ### FOR THE MAN
> ### WHO WORKS HARD.

Dear Lord.
*   Help me to be diligent and to work hard*
in everything I do.
                    Amen.

DISCERNMENT

SOME OF THE BRIGHTEST STARS in football also have the most discernment about what is really important in the game of life. Often players on both teams gather in group prayer at mid-field after games. 2001 Super Bowl champion Trent Dilfer said, "Football or anything we do in our day-to-day lives should be an act of worship to Him. So that should be our logical response—to kneel on the field and pray in thanksgiving or need, or giving up ourselves in a time of great stress. In a time when the world's looking at us to be superstars, we've simply saying, 'God, this isn't about me. This is about You.'"

APPLICATION

EVERY CHRISTIAN needs discernment to know what is true and what is false. We hear so many conflicting ideas today that we must discern what is from God and what comes from Satan. The Bible says we are to discern good from evil, right from wrong, and the best from what is less than the best.

DEFINITIONS:

Discernment — "Keen perception or judgment, insight."

Wisdom — "The ability to use knowledge."

"Mocker — "One who scoffs, ridicules, or disappoints."

Folly — "Foolish ideas, words, or deeds."

Rebuke — "To reprimand or point out fault."

CHARACTER CALISTHENICS:

What is the Relationship of Discernment to Wisdom?

_____ is found on the lips of the _____ , but a _____ is for the back of him who lacks _____ .

Proverbs 10:13

_____ reposes in the _____ of the _____ and even among _____ she lets herself be known.

Proverbs 14:33

A _____ man keeps _____ in view, but a fool's _____ wander to the ends of the _____ .

Proverbs 17:24

What is the Relationship
of Discernment to Knowledge?

The _____ seeks _____ and
finds none, but _____ comes easily to
the _____ .

Proverbs 14:6

The _____ heart seeks _____ ,
but the mouth of a _____ feeds on _____ .

Proverbs 15:14

The _____ of the discerning acquires
_____ ; the ears of the _____
seek it out.

Proverbs 18:15

How Does Correction Affect the Discerning Person?

A rebuke_____ a man of _____
more than a _____ lashes a _____ .

Proverbs 17:10

Flog a _____ , and the simple will learn
_____ ; rebuke a discerning man,
and he will gain _____ .

Proverbs 19:25

SHORT SPRINTS:

    1. A discerning person speaks wisdom (Proverbs 10:13).   T   F

    2. Fools feed on knowledge (Proverbs 15:14).   T   F

    3. A poor man with discernment sees through a rich
        man (Proverbs 28:11).   T   F

MIND STRETCHERS:

    How can you be more discerning in situations at school?

    At home?

In sports?

Who is the most discerning person you know?

How can you be more like him/her?

STRENGTHEN YOUR GRIP:
Write out Proverbs 3:21, 22:

_____

_____

_____

_____

_____

> **A DISCERNING PERSON THINKS AHEAD**
> **ABOUT EACH DECISION**
> **AND IS SURE TO CHOOSE GOD'S WAY**
> **AND NOT HIS OWN.**

Dear Lord,
   Help me to discern your ways.
                              Amen.

DISCIPLINE

HAMILTON-BROWN, a boxer from South Africa, suffered the consequences of an undisciplined lifestyle after his bout in the 1936 Olympics. Declared the loser in a split decision, Hamilton-Brown tried to ease his pain by going on an eating binge. Hours later, officials found a scoring error and gave him the victory. But his lack of self-control had caused him to gain five pounds. He was over the weight limit and was disqualified the following day!

APPLICATION

A DISCIPLINED LIFESTYLE is not only important in athletics, but also in every area of life. Without discipline, we lose many benefits we might have gained, including both self-respect and the blessing of God.

DEFINITIONS:

Discipline — "Training that produces orderliness, obedience, and self-control."

Knowledge — "Information that may be known."

Understanding — "Intelligence."

Folly — "Foolish actions or ideas."

CHARACTER CALISTHENICS:

Why Were the Proverbs Written?

For attaining _____ and _____ ; for _____ words of insight; for acquiring a _____ and _____ life, doing what is _____ and _____ and _____ .

Proverbs 1:2, 3

What Should Be Our Attitude Toward Discipline?

My son, do not _____ the Lord's _____ and do not _____ his rebuke, because the LORD _____ those he _____ as a _____ the son he _____ in.

Proverbs 3:11, 12

He who _____ discipline comes to _____ and _____ , but whoever _____ correction is _____ .

Proverbs 13:18

He who _____ discipline _____ himself, but whoever _____ correction gains _____ .

Proverbs 15:32

How Does Love Relate to a Father's Discipline of His Children?

_____ your son, for in that there is
_____ ; do not be a _____ party to
his _____ .

Proverbs 19:18

_____ is bound up in the _____
of a _____ , but the _____ of _____
will drive it far from him.

Proverbs 22:15

Do not _____ discipline from a _____ :
if you _____ him with the _____ ,
he will not die.

Proverbs 23:13

SHORT SPRINTS:

1. If parents do not spank children when they need it, they do not love them (Proverbs 13:24). T   F
2. Spanking a child will save him from death (Proverbs 23:14). T   F
3. God disciplines those he loves (Proverbs 3:12). T   F

MIND STRETCHERS:

How have you been disciplined by your parents?

By God?

How do you need to live a more disciplined life at home?

At school?

In your sport?

STRENGTHEN YOUR GRIP:
Write out Proverbs 12:1:

_____

_____

_____

DISCIPLINE COMES FROM GOD AND IS OFTEN SENT THROUGH OUR PARENTS. NO ONE EVER BECAME AN OUTSTANDING PERSON WITHOUT DISCIPLINE.

Dear Lord,
Help me to live a more disciplined life.
Amen.

DISCRETION

RACE CAR DRIVER LLOYD RUBY failed to use discretion in the 1969
Indianapolis 500 and it ended the race for him. In the lead on the 105th
lap, he stopped to refuel. But he became so impatient, he took off while
the fuel hose was still in the tank fitting and ripped the left side off his
thin-skinned car! The entire fuel tank went with the side of the car!
Because he failed to use discretion, the race became history in a hurry
for Lloyd Ruby.

APPLICATION

WHEN WE FAIL to use discretion in our decisions and our actions, we suffer
in the "race" of life. Let's see what God says about using sound judgment and
discretion.

DEFINITIONS:

Prudence — "Careful,
discreet, showing
forethought."

Discretion — "Careful-
ness about what one
does or says; pru-
dence."

Insight — "Mental
penetration into prob-
lems."

CHARACTER CALISTHENICS:

What are the Reasons Solomon
Wrote the Proverbs?

For giving _____ to the _____ ,
_____ and _____ to the
young.

Proverbs 1:4

How Can We Maintain Discretion?

My son, pay _____ to my _____ ,
_____ well to my words of _____ ,
that you may maintain _____ and
your lips may preserve _____ .

Proverbs 5:1, 2

Who Do We Resemble
When We Lack Discretion?

Like a gold _____ in a pig's _____ is a
_____ woman who shows no
_____ .

Proverbs 11:22

SHORT SPRINTS:

1. Wisdom helps us maintain discretion
   (Proverbs 5:2).   T   F
2. Discretion is not important when one is young
   (Proverbs 1:4).   T   F
3. Lack of discretion degrades a beautiful woman
   (Proverbs 11:22).   T   F

MIND STRETCHERS:

What does using discretion mean to you in your school life?

At home?

In athletics?

Who is a good example of discretion?

STRENGTHEN YOUR GRIP:

Write out Proverbs 2:11:

_____

_____

_____

_____

> **WE GAIN DISCRETION AND SAVE OURSELVES FROM MANY PROBLEMS WHEN WE LISTEN TO AND OBEY GOD'S WORD.**

Dear Lord,
Help me to use discretion in every decision.
Amen.

ENDURANCE (Perseverance)

THE 20-KILOMETER WALK is an Olympic event that usually attracts little attention. But the event at the 1984 Los Angeles games provided an exception. Early in the race, an athlete from El Salvador fell significantly behind. The participants walked five laps, excited the stadium, and walked the streets of Los Angeles for 2 1/2 hours before returning for the finish. When the other walkers left the stadium, the participant from El Salvador still had three laps to go! Everyone thought he would take the nearest exit and quit in disgrace. When it became apparent to the crowd that he was staying in the race, people began to clap for him, then chant "El Salvador" as they stood each time he passed. The 10,000 meter run was the next race and it was begun. Soon, the walker from El Salvador entered the stadium! Everyone's attention was turned to him as he crossed the finish line and collapsed. The trauma wagon picked him up and drove a victory lap around the coliseum to the cheers of the crowd. He had persevered to the end and he was loved for it!

APPLICATION

GOD EXPECTS His children to endure to the end. We are to stay in the race no matter what the obstacles, walking each step by faith. We are to cross the finish line of the race marked out for us. Jesus is our Example.

DEFINITIONS:

Endurance — "Staying with a task no matter how long it takes."

CHARACTER CALISTHENICS:

What Did Jesus Endure?

Let us fix our _____ on Jesus, the _____ and_____ of our faith, who for the _____ set before him _____ the cross, _____ its shame, and sat down at the right hand of the throne of God. Consider him who _____ such _____ from sinful men, so that you will not grow _____ and lose heart.

Hebrews 12:2, 3

As Soldiers of Jesus Christ, What Must We Endure Patiently?

Endure _____ with us like a good _____ of Christ Jesus.

2 Timothy 2:3

Evangelist — "A person who preaches the gospel."

But you, keep your _____ in all _____ , endure _____ , do the work of an _____ , discharge all the duties of your _____ .

2 Timothy 4:5

Ministry — "Service to others."

Blessed is the man who _____ under _____ , because when he has stood the _____ , he will receive the _____ of life that God has promised to those who love him.

James 1:12

Discipline — "Child training."

What Things Do Not Endure?

For _____ do not _____ forever, and a _____ is not secure for all generations.

Proverbs 27:24

SHORT SPRINTS:

1. God's love endures forever (Psalm 100:5). T F
2. Sometimes love doesn't persevere (1 Corinthians 13:7). T F
3. Christians must persevere through trial
   (2 Thessalonians 1:4). T F

MIND STRETCHERS:

Who is an example of endurance to you?

What must you endure in school?

In sports?

STRENGTHEN YOUR GRIP:
Write out Hebrews 12:7:

_____

_____

_____

_____

GOD GIVES THE CROWN OF LIFE
TO THOSE WHO ENDURE UNDER TRIAL.

Dear Lord,
Help me to endure every trial that comes my way.
Amen.

FAITHFULNESS (Loyalty)

PRIOR TO LEAVING for the 1972 Olympics in Munich, Germany, the U.S. Wrestling team stopped in Washington, D.C., for a special tour of the White House. As they prepared to begin the tour, the manager noticed that Dan Gable, Ben Peterson, and John Peterson were missing. When he found them and asked why they were not going to the White House they replied, "We are headed to Munich to win medals, so we're going to work out." Their faithfulness to their cause paid off when Dan and Ben won gold medals and John won a silver medal.

APPLICATION

HOW CHRISTIANS would please God if they were as faithful to Him as these Olympic wrestlers were to their purpose! His faithfulness to us should motivate our loyalty to Him. Let's examine what He says about loyalty and faithfulness.

DEFINITIONS:

Loyalty — "Faithfulness to a person, cause, or duty."

CHARACTER CALISTHENICS:

What Should Be Our Attitude Concerning Faithfulness to Our God?

Let _____ and _____ never leave you; _____ them around your _____ , write them on the tablet of your _____ .

Proverbs 3:3

What Are the Results of Faithfulness?

Then you will win _____ and a good _____ in the sight of _____ and _____ .

Proverbs 3:4

What Does God Promise to His Faithful Ones?

A _____ man will be richly _____ , but one eager to get rich will not go _____ .

Proverbs 28:20

_____ the Lord, all his saints! The Lord _____the _____ , but the _____ he pays back in full.

Psalm 31:23

What Traits Do Trustworthy Men Possess?

A _____ betrays a confidence, but a _____ man keeps a secret.

Proverbs 11:13

A _____ messenger falls into _____, but a _____ envoy brings _____ .

Proverbs 13:17

Gossip — "One who talks about others with no intent to help."

Envoy — "Messenger."

SHORT SPRINTS:

1. A faithful man is hard to find (Proverbs 20:6).   T   F
2. Jesus is our faithful witness about the nature of God
   (Revelation 1:5).   T   F
3. God's faithfulness continues through all generations
   (Psalm 119:90).   T   F

MIND STRETCHERS:

Who is faithful to you?

Are you faithful to your family?

Your school?

Your friends?

Your team?

Your church?

STRENGTHEN YOUR GRIP:
    Write out Revelation 2:10:

_____

_____

_____

_____

> **THE FAITHFULNESS OF JESUS TO US AND TO GOD CAUSES US TO WANT TO BE FAITHFUL TO HIM.**

Dear Lord,
Help me to be faithful.
Amen.

FEAR OF THE LORD

SCIENTISTS SAY that between 2,500 and 10,000 small earthquakes ripple our planet every day. Most are small tremors, but everyone remembers the October 17, 1989 quake that interrupted the World Series in San Francisco. An even bigger quake hit southern Missouri in 1812 and changed the course of the Mississippi River. And a huge earthquake in China in 1976 killed almost 400,000 people. These tremors shake our confidence in the very ground we walk on and bring fear to the hearts of men.

APPLICATION

THERE IS ANOTHER kind of fear we must have in our hearts if we are to honor God. The "fear of the Lord" means we have a healthy respect for Him. It results in our trust, worship, and obedience to His commands.

DEFINITIONS:

Fear (of the Lord) — "respect for who God is and what He can do."

Commands — "orders from a higher authority."

Wisdom — "seeing things from God's perspective."

Understanding — "Comprehension."

CHARACTER CALISTHENICS:

How Do We Learn the Fear of the Lord?

My son, if you _____ my words and _____ up my _____ within you, _____ your ear to _____ and _____ your heart to _____ , and if you _____ out for _____ and _____ aloud for _____ and if you _____ for it as for silver and _____ for it as for hidden treasure, then you will _____ the _____ of the Lord and _____ the _____ of God.

Proverbs 2:1-5

How Important is the Fear of the Lord?

The _____ of the Lord is the _____ of _____ , but _____ despise _____ and _____ .

Proverbs 1:7

The _____ of the Lord is the _____
of _____ and _____ of the
Holy One is _____ .

Proverbs 9:10

The _____ of the Lord adds _____ to
_____ .

Proverbs 10:27

What are the Results of Fearing God?

Through _____ and _____ sin is
atoned for; through the _____ of the Lord a man
avoids _____ .

Proverbs 16:6

He who _____ the Lord has a _____
fortress, and for his _____
it will be a _____ . The fear of the
Lord is a _____ of _____ ,
turning a man from the _____ of _____ .

Proverbs 14:26, 27

The _____ of the Lord leads to _____ ;
then one rests _____ , untouched by
_____ .

Proverbs 19:23

Fool — "One who has no respect for God or His power."

Discipline — "Enforced righteousness."

Shuns — "Avoids."

Secure — "Not able to be overthrown."

Refuge — "A place of safety."

Snares — "Traps."

Content — "Satisfied."

SHORT SPRINTS:

1. To fear the Lord is to love evil (Proverbs 8:13).   T   F
2. A wise man fears the Lord and shuns evil
   (Proverbs 14:16).   T   F
3. The fear of the Lord teaches a man humility
   (Proverbs 15:33).   T   F

MIND STRETCHERS:

Why is it wise to fear God?

How do our actions show that we fear God?

STRENGTHEN YOUR GRIP:

Write out Proverbs 28:14:

_____

_____

_____

_____

> ### TO FEAR GOD MEANS WE NEED NOT FEAR ANYTHING OR ANYONE ELSE IN THIS WORLD.

Dear Lord,
    Help me to show the fear of the Lord by the
way I live.

                                        Amen.

FRIENDSHIP

CHARLES DAVIS was 13 years old when Freddy, age 17, wanted him to break into a building and steal some typewriters. The older boy said he would be a lookout. Young Charles thought it over and told Freddy, "You go in. I'm going home."

Six years later, Charles was a star basketball player for Vanderbilt University and he visited the state prison. There he saw Freddy for the first time since that night. He had been in prison since they had last met. "If I had gone in that building and got caught, who knows what would have happened to me," says Charles, who played eight years in the NBA.

APPLICATION

CHARLES DAVIS made a wise choice to get away from Freddy. His life could have ended in disaster if he had chosen otherwise. Let's see what God's Word says about the friends we choose.

DEFINITIONS:

Righteous — "In right standing with God."

Cautious — "Moving with an awareness of danger."

Companion — "One with whom you hang around."

Fool — "One who has no use for God or His laws."

Drunkard — "One addicted to alcohol."

Glutton — "One who can't control his eating habits."

CHARACTER CALISTHENICS:

What Should Be Our Attitude in Seeking Friends?

A _____ man is _____ in friendship, but the way of the _____ leads them _____ .

Proverbs 12:26

What Kind of Friends Should We Seek?

He who walks with the _____ grows _____ , but a _____ of _____ suffers harm.

Proverbs 13:20

What Kind of People Should We Not Select as Friends?

Do not _____ those who drink too much _____ or _____ themselves on _____ , for _____ and _____ become _____ and drowsiness clothes them in _____ .

Proverbs 23:20

Do not envy _____ men, do not desire
their _____ ; for their hearts plot
_____ , and their lips talk about
making _____ .

                                    Proverbs 24:1, 2
Stay away from a _____ man, for you
will not find _____ on his lips.
                                    Proverbs 14:7

SHORT SPRINTS:

1. Gossip separates close friends (Proverbs 16:28).   T   F
2. It is okay to be friends with hot-tempered people
    (Proverbs 22:24).   T   F
3. Fickle friends avoid a poor person (Proverbs 19:4).   T   F

MIND STRETCHERS:

Who is your best friend?

Why is he/she loyal?

How can you make a good friend?

STRENGTHEN YOUR GRIP:
    Write out Proverbs 18:24:

_____

_____

_____

_____

JESUS IS A FRIEND WHO STICKS CLOSER THAN A BROTHER.

Dear Lord,
    Help me make friends with those who honor you.
                     Amen.

GENEROSITY

YANKEE RIGHTFIELDER Roger Maris broke Babe Ruth's record by hitting 61 home runs in 1961. Nineteen-year-old Sal Durante rose from his rightfield seat, reached as high as he could, and caught the ball. Durante was later ushered to the clubhouse to meet Maris and he tried to give it to him. "No, you keep it," said Roger. "Try to make some money off it."

Durante sold the ball to a restaurant owner who then gave it to Maris.

APPLICATION

ROGER MARIS was generous in not immediately claiming the ball from a 19-year-old kid. His attitude was different from the greed we see so much in sports today. Let's see what the Bible says about our own attitudes toward money and possessions.

DEFINITIONS:

Poverty — "Not having enough."

Prosper — "Have plenty."

Generous — "One who gives freely."

Greedy — "self-seeking."

Bribes — "illegal payments for special favors."

CHARACTER CALISTHENICS:

What is God's Promise to Generous People?

One man gives _____ , yet _____ even more; another _____ unduly, but comes to _____ .

Proverbs 11:24

A _____ man will himself be _____ , for he _____ his food with the _____ .

Proverbs 22:9

What Are the Consequences of Greed?

A _____ man brings _____ to his family, but he who hates _____ will live.

Proverbs 15:27

A _____ man stirs up _____ , but he who _____ in the Lord will _____ .

Proverbs 28:25

He who _____ to the _____ will
lack _____ , but he who closes his
_____ to them receives many _____ .
                                                    Proverbs 28:27

Dissention — "argu-
ments."

What is the Result of Gift-Giving?
Many curry _____ with a ruler, and everyone is the _____ of a man who gives

_____ .
                                                    Proverbs 19:6

Curse — "A wish of evil
against a person."

A _____ opens the way for the _____
and ushers him into the _____ of the great.
                                                    Proverbs 18:16

SHORT SPRINTS:
1. A poor, suffering person can still be generous
   (2 Corinthians 8:2).   T   F
2. God gives wisdom generously to all who ask (James 1:5). T   F
3. Some boast of giving gifts they do not give
   (Proverbs 25:14).   T   F

MIND STRETCHERS:
Who is the most generous person you know?

How can you be more generous at school?

At home?

In athletics?

STRENGTHEN YOUR GRIP:
Write out Proverbs 11:25:

_____

_____

_____

_____

> **JESUS SAID
> IT IS BETTER TO GIVE
> THAN TO RECEIVE.**

Dear Lord,
Help me to be generous today.
Amen.

GOAL-ORIENTED

SPORT PSYCHOLOGIST Thomas Tutko has helped many major league hitters overcome the mental obstacles that rob them of confidence at the plate. Tutko stresses the importance of *concentrating on the immediate task at hand.* In this way a player is not distracted and his efforts are not divided. Rather than worrying about success and failure, the hitter must "calmly swing, relax, think about what he's trying to do, and thoughts of failure or success will be pushed out of his head by the business at hand." In other words, a single goal is needed. The mind must have a goal, but it must be one single goal at a time.

APPLICATION

ANYONE WHO has ever achieved anything has had a goal and has planned how to reach that goal. We must plan in a definite direction and act accordingly, counting on God to direct us. After all, to aim at nothing means we'll hit it every time! What does God say about goals, plans, and success?

DEFINITIONS:

Victory — "Success."

Treasure — "That which is of value to you."

CHARACTER CALISTHENICS:

Who Should We Include in Making Plans?

Instead, you ought to say, "If it is the Lord's _____ , we will live and do _____ or _____ ."

James 4:15

Plans fail for lack of _____ , but with many _____ they _____ .

Proverbs 15:22

For waging war you need _____ , and for _____ many _____ .

Proverbs 24:6

Who Determines All Our Success?

In his heart a man _____ his course, but the _____ determines his _____ .

Proverbs 16:9

Many are the _____ in a man's _____ ,
but it is the _____ purpose that _____ .

Proverbs 19:21

A man's _____ are directed by the _____ .
How then can anyone _____ his own
way?

Proverbs 20:24

What Priorities Did Jesus Give Us
in Setting Goals and Making Plans?

Do not store up for yourselves _____
on _____ , where moth and rust _____
and where _____ break in and _____ .
But store up for yourselves _____
in _____ , where moth and rust
do not _____ , and where _____ do
not break in and steal. For where your _____ is,
there your _____ will be also.

Matthew 6:19-21

SHORT SPRINTS:

    1. No plan succeeds against the Lord (Proverbs 21:30).   T   F

    2. Victory comes from man (Proverbs 21:31).   T   F

    3. Your heart is where you put your values (Matthew 6:21). T   F

MIND STRETCHERS:

    What goals have you set in school?

In sports?

On the job?

STRENGTHEN YOUR GRIP:
Write out Proverbs 16:3:

_____

_____

_____

_____

> ## SET WISE GOALS
> ## AND WORK HARD
> ## TO REACH THEM.

Dear Lord,
Help me to set Godly goals.
Amen.

HONESTY

WHILE PREPARING a 9-inch putt in a tournament offering a top prize of $108,000, Ray Floyd saw the ball move ever so slightly. According to the rules, if the ball moves in this way the golfer must take a penalty stroke. The temptation is great to pass it off and hope nobody saw it. But Ray Floyd didn't do that. He charged himself with a penalty stroke and ended up with a bogey on the hole.

APPLICATION

HONESTY is always the best policy, whether or not those around us are honest.

DEFINITIONS:

Abhors — "Hates."

Fraud — "Deceit."

Detests — "Despises."

CHARACTER CALISTHENICS:

What Does God Think of Honesty in Business?

The Lord _____ dishonest _____ ,
but _____ weights are his _____ .

Proverbs 11:1

Differing _____ and differing _____
— the Lord _____ them both.

Proverbs 20:10

The Lord _____ lying _____ , but
he _____ in men who are _____ .

Proverbs 12:22

How Does a Truthful Man Differ from a Liar?

A _____ witness does not _____ ,
but a _____ witness pours out _____ .

Proverbs 14:5

A _____ witness _____ lives,
but a _____ witness is _____ .

Proverbs 14:25

What is the End Result of Lying and Flattery?

A _____ witness will not go _____ ,
and he who pours out _____ will not go
_____ .

Proverbs 19:5

A _____ witness will _____ , and whoever _____ to him will be _____ forever.

Proverbs 21:28

A _____ tongue _____ those it hurts, and a _____ mouth works _____ .

Proverbs 26:28

Flattery — "Saying nice things for the purpose of deceiving someone."

SHORT SPRINTS:
1. Food gained by fraud tastes sweet at first (Proverbs 20:17). T   F
2. A king's rule is established through righteousness (Proverbs 16:12).   T   F
3. Good kings value truth (Proverbs 16:13).   T   F

MIND STRETCHERS:
Who is the most honest person you know?

Is it ever right to lie?

STRENGTHEN YOUR GRIP:
Write out Proverbs 16:11:

_____

_____

_____

_____

_____

50 • HONESTY

**THE TRUTH WINS IN THE END.
THEREFORE, MAKE FRIENDS WITH THE TRUTH.
IF WE ARE HONEST, TRUTH IS OUR BEST FRIEND.
IF WE ARE DISHONEST, TRUTH IS OUR GREATEST ENEMY.**

Dear Lord,
Help me to be an honest person.
Amen.

HONOR

ERIC LIDDELL was the 100 meter sprint champion of the world in 1924. Because of his conviction that he should honor God by not running on Sunday, Eric was left out of his event in Paris' Olympic Games. Instead, he ran the 400 meter on the following Wednesday. A trainer gave him a piece of paper with this verse just prior to the race: "Those that honor me, I will honor" (1 Samuel 2:30). Eric won the race! Later, he gave up fame and fortune to go as an unknown missionary to China. During WWII, Eric was a prisoner of war and led recreation exercises in prison. He died at the age of 41 without seeing his third son who was born there.

APPLICATION

ERIC LIDDELL honored God on earth and God blessed him both on earth and in heaven. As we learn from his story, there is sometimes a cost to honoring God.

DEFINITIONS:

Shame — "Disgrace."

Pride — "Self-centered conceit."

Disdained — "Brought down."

CHARACTER CALISTHENICS:

Who Gains Honor?

The _____ inherit honor, but _____ he holds up to _____ .

Proverbs 3:35

A man's _____ brings him _____ , but a man of _____ spirit gains _____ .

Proverbs 29:23

Those that _____ me, I will _____ , but those who _____ me will be _____ .

1 Samuel 2:30

What Comes Before Honor?

The _____ of the _____ teaches a man _____ , and _____ comes before _____ .

Proverbs 15:33

What Does an Honorable Person Avoid?

It is to a man's _____ to avoid _____ ,
but every _____ is quick to _____ .

Proverbs 20:3

Strife — "Bitter and continuous controversy."

It is not good to eat too much _____ , nor is it
_____ to seek one's own _____ .

Proverbs 25:27

Who Does Not Deserve Honor?

Like _____ in summer or _____
in harvest, _____ is not fitting for a fool.

Proverbs 26:1

Fool — "One who has no heart for truth."

Like tying a stone in a sling is the giving of _____
to a _____ .

Proverbs 26:8

How is an Honorable Man Tested?

The crucible for silver and the furnace for gold, but a
man is _____ by the _____ he
receives.

Proverbs 27:21

Praise — "Good comments."

SHORT SPRINTS:

1. Wisdom brings honor (Proverbs 4:8).   T   F
2. Honor comes before humility (Proverbs 18:12).   T   F
3. We must honor our parents (Exodus 20:12).   T   F

MIND STRETCHERS:

Who is worthy of special honor?

How do you honor them?

STRENGTHEN YOUR GRIP:
Write out Proverbs 13:18:

_____

_____

_____

_____

IF YOU HONOR GOD
IN YOUR WORDS AND DEEDS,
HE WILL HONOR YOU WITH BLESSING.

Dear Lord,
Help me to honor you above all.
Amen.

HOPE

TAILBACK OTIS MOUNDS had no hope of getting in the game as a freshman at Auburn University. Otis had suffered a hamstring injury and coach Pat Dye planned to redshirt him. So, he attended Auburn's 1990 home-opener against Fullerton State as a fan. Mounds cheered Auburn's first touchdown and thought nothing of it when the starting tailback left the game with an ankle injury. But when the second-string tailback was injured in the second quarter, he started to wonder what the coach would do. Sure enough, as Otis watched the half-time show from the upper deck, the public address announcer said: "Will Otis Mounds please report to the Auburn locker room."

Sprinting through the crowd, he found coach Dye waiting with a jersey. His hopes were rekindled and by the end of the game Otis Mounds had carried the ball five times for 33 yards in a 38-17 victory! Not bad for a guy who had no hope of playing when the game began.

APPLICATION

GOD IS GOOD to us. He is a God who is noted for restoring hope in hopeless situations. It is God who gives us a reason to have hope in the future.

DEFINITIONS:

Deferred — "Post-poned."

Fool — "A rebel against God and His laws."

Detest — "Hate se-verely."

CHARACTER CALISTHENICS:

How Do We Feel When a Longing is Fulfilled?

A _____ fulfilled is _____ to the _____ , but _____ detest _____ from _____ .

Proverbs 13:19

What Gives Us Hope for the Future?

Know also that _____ is _____ to your soul; if you find it there is a future _____ for you, and your _____ will not be _____ off.

Proverbs 24:14

Who Has Not Future Hope?

The _____ man has no _____ hope, and the _____ of the _____ will be snuffed out.

Proverbs 24:20

The prospect of the _____ is _____, but the _____ of the _____ come to _____ .

Proverbs 10:28

Do you see a man _____ in his _____ eyes? There is more _____ for a _____ than for him.

Proverbs 26:12

When a _____ man dies, his _____ perishes; all he _____ from his power comes to _____ .

Proverbs 11:7

Righteous — "Those in right standing with God."

SHORT SPRINTS:

1. There is little hope for a man who speaks in haste (Proverbs 29:20).   T   F
2. Our hope is in God (Psalm 39:7).   T   F
3. We should hope in God's Word (Psalm 119:114).   T   F

MIND STRETCHERS:

In whom is your hope for the present?

For the future?

STRENGTHEN YOUR GRIP:
Write out Proverbs 13:12:

_____

_____

_____

_____

> # OUR HOPE IS BUILT
> # ON NOTHING LESS
> # THAN JESUS'
> # BLOOD AND RIGHTEOUSNESS

Dear Lord,
*   I hope in You for all I need. Do not let me*
be disappointed.

Amen.

HUMILITY

DESIGNATED HITTER DON BAYLOR was a star for the 1986 Boston Red Sox. Though passed over as a pinch hitter of Game 6 of the World Series that year, he didn't yield to the temptation to feel sorry for himself. While he was disappointed, Baylor simply said, "That's the way the game is played." Such humility enabled the Red Sox to enjoy a great year when they were predicted to be a minor factor in the pennant race.

APPLICATION

ARROGANT PRIDE is the opposite of humility. If Don Baylor had let pride rule his life, he would have created a problem for the Red Sox. That's why humility is so important.

DEFINITIONS:

Grace — "First class conduct."

Pride — "Self-centered arrogance."

Disgrace — "Lack of class."

Detests — "Hates."

Oppressed — "Put down."

CHARACTER CALISTHENICS:

What Does God Give to the Humble?

He mocks _____ mockers but gives _____ to the _____ .

Proverbs 3:34

When _____ comes, then comes _____ , but with _____ comes _____ .

Proverbs 11:2

The _____ of the Lord teaches a man wisdom, and _____ comes before _____ .

Proverbs 15:33

What Does God Promise for the Proud?

The Lord detests all the _____ of heart. Be sure of this: They will _____ go _____ .

Proverbs 16:5

Pride goes before _____ , a _____ spirit before a _____ . Better to be _____ in spirit and among the _____ than to share _____ with the _____ .

Proverbs 16:18, 19

Before his _____ a man's heart is _____,
but _____ comes before _____.

Proverbs 18:12

What Are Characteristics of Pride?

The _____ and _____ man —
"Mocker" is his name; he behaves with overweening
_____ .

Proverbs 21:24

Do not _____ about tomorrow, for you do not
know what a _____ may bring forth. Let another
_____ you and not your own _____;
someone else, and not your own _____ .

Proverbs 27:1, 2

Plunder — "Goods taken in war."

Overweening — "overbearing."

Boast — "Brag."

Exalted — "Lifted up."

SHORT SPRINTS:

1. A proud heart is sinful (Proverbs 21:4).   T   F
2. A fool exalts himself (Proverbs 30:32).   T   F
3. Wisdom hates pride and arrogance (Proverbs 8:13).   T   F

MIND STRETCHERS:

Who is the most humble person you know at school?

On your team?

STRENGTHEN YOUR GRIP:

Write out James 4:10:

_____

_____

_____

_____

OUR ROLE IS TO HUMBLE OURSELVES.
GOD'S ROLE IS TO LIFT US UP.
IF WE DO HIS JOB, HE'LL DO OURS!

Dear Lord,
I humble myself before You.
Amen.

INTEGRITY

THE RULES OF GOLF are very precise and many good golfers are tempted to bend them. In 1987, Craig Stadler placed a towel on the ground before hitting a shot from beneath a tree. He said it was to keep his slacks clean, but he was declared in violation of Rule 13-2 which prohibits "building a stance." The penalty cost him $37,000.

In 1991, Paul Azinger disturbed a small stone in the Doral Ryder Open. He was cited for "moving a loose impediment lying in . . . the hazard," and disqualified for signing an incorrect scorecard.

One golfer known for his impeccable integrity was Bobby Jones. Years ago, Bobby called a one-stroke penalty on himself, causing him to lose the U.S. Open by a single stroke! When praised for his honesty, he said, "There is only one way to play the game. You might as well praise a man for not robbing a bank."

APPLICATION

GOD WANTS all His children to live with integrity. He expects us to be honest in the small things as well as the big things.

DEFINITIONS:

Integrity — "Moral reliability."

Duplicity — "Double-mindedness; thinking both good and evil toward others."

CHARACTER CALISTHENICS:

What Benefits Belong to a Person Who Lives with Integrity?

The _____ of the upright _____ them, but the unfaithful are _____ by their duplicity.

Proverbs 11:3

Righteousness _____ the man of integrity, but wickedness _____ the sinner.

Proverbs 13:6

How Do Evil Men Act Toward a Person Who Has Integrity?

Bloodthirsty men _____ a man of integrity and seek to _____ the upright.

Proverbs 29:10

SHORT SPRINTS:

1. Despite his sins, David led Israel with integrity of heart and skillful hands (Psalm 78:72).   T   F
2. Job maintained his integrity despite severe suffering (Job 2:3).   T   F
3. Integrity makes a difference when God judges his people (Psalm 7:8).   T   F

MIND STRETCHERS:

Who do you respect for his/her integrity?

How do you demonstrate integrity in school?

At home?

On the playing field?

STRENGTHEN YOUR GRIP:

Write out Proverbs 10:9:

_____

_____

_____

_____

> **HONESTY IS NOT ONLY THE BEST POLICY, BUT FOR THE CHRISTIAN IT IS THE ONLY POLICY.**

Dear Lord,
> *Help me to be morally reliable.*
>> *Amen.*

JOYFUL

THE JOY OF THE WORLD is dependent upon outward circumstances. Any athletic team has great joy when they win a championship — especially when they win unexpectedly. The incredible joy of Bobby Thompson and the Giants following his home run to win the 1951 National League pennant is an example. So is Bill Mazeroski's seventh game, bottom of the ninth home run to give the Pirates victory in the 1960 World Series and Kirk Gibson's shot to win Game 1 of the 1988 Series. These heroics give "goosebumps" to all true fans.

APPLICATION

A CHRISTIAN HAS constant joy that is not dependent upon positive, outward circumstances. Christians who are walking close to God have joyful hearts no matter what happens to them! In contrast, what the world calls "joy" is better named "happiness." It comes and goes, depending upon external factors.

DEFINITIONS:

Joy — "A very good inner feeling no matter what the circumstances."

CHARACTER CALISTHENICS:

How Can Joy be Spread to Others?

A _____ look brings _____ to the _____ , and _____ news gives _____ to the _____ .

Proverbs 15:30

What Does our Inner Heart Have to do with our Faces?

A _____ heart makes the face _____ , but _____ crushes the _____ .

Proverbs 15:13

How Does a Cheerful Heart Affect our Health?

A _____ heart is good _____ , but a _____ spirit dries up the _____ .

Proverbs 17:22

Where Does Joy Come From?

But the fruit of the _____ is _____ ,

_____ , _____ , _____ ,

_____ , _____ , _____ ,

_____ , and _____ .

Galatians 5:22, 23

SHORT SPRINTS:

    1. There is joy for the father of a fool (Proverbs 17:21).   T   F

    2. Justice brings joy to the righteous (Proverbs 21:15).   T   F

    3. The father of the wise has great joy (Proverbs 15:20).   T   F

MIND STRETCHERS:

Who is the most joyful person you know?

What gives you the most joy?

STRENGTHEN YOUR GRIP:

Write out Nehemiah 8:10:

_____

_____

_____

_____

> **JOY IS SPELLED:**
> ## JESUS
> ### OTHERS
> #### YOU
> **IN THAT ORDER.**
> **WHEN WE PUT OURSELVES THIRD,**
> **WE HAVE JOY.**

Dear Lord,

Restore to me the joy of my salvation.

Amen.

JUSTICE

INTEGRITY with honest effort are the foundation stones of college basketball. That's why swift justice must be served when players are proven guilty of giving less than their best for money from gamblers (point-shaving).

In 1951, two Manhatten College players and three gamblers were arrested for "fixing" games. Kentucky coach Adolph Rupp called it a big city problem. "They couldn't touch my boys with a 10-foot pole," he proclaimed. However, after winning the 1951 NCAA Tournament and being ranked #1 in 1952, his program was shut down, stained by a national scandel that involved seven schools and 32 players. Justice was served on the criminals involved, though it took many years for college basketball to recover.

APPLICATION

IT IS EXTREMELY important for those in authority to punish evildoers. And it is equally important to reward the righteous.

DEFINITIONS:

Innocent — "Not guilty."

Flog — "To whip."

Integrity — "Moral uprightness."

Aquitting — "Declaring one not guilty."

Condemning — "Declaring a person guilty."

CHARACTER CALISTHENICS:

What Does God Expect of those in Authority Concerning Justice?

It is not _____ to _____ an innocent man, or to _____ officials for their

_____ .

Proverbs 17:26

It is not good to be _____ to the _____ or to deprive the _____ of _____ .

Proverbs 18:5

Aquitting the _____ and _____ the _____ — the Lord _____ them both.

Proverbs 17:15

What are the Advantages of a Just Government?

To show _____ in judging is not _____ ;
whoever says to the _____ , "You are
_____ " — peoples will _____
him and nations _____ him. But
it will go _____ with those who _____
the _____ , and rich _____
will come upon them.

Proverbs 24:23- 25

By _____ a king gives a country _____ ,
but one who is _____ for _____
tears it down.

Proverbs 29:4

If a king _____ the poor with _____ ,
his throne will always be _____ .

Proverbs 29:14

Partiality — "Favorit-ism."

Convict — "To find guilty."

Bribe — "Money paid in secret for a special deed."

Pervert — "To under-mine or destroy."

SHORT SPRINTS:

1. It is good to be partial in judging (Proverbs 24:23).   T   F
2. The righteous care about justice for the poor
   (Proverbs 29:7).   T   F
3. A bribe perverts justice (Proverbs 17:23).   T   F

MIND STRETCHERS:

Where have you seen justice in school?

On your team?

Where have you seen injustice?

How did you feel?

STRENGTHEN YOUR GRIP:

Write out Micah 6:8:

_____

_____

_____

_____

> ### ACT JUSTLY, LOVE MERCY,
> ### AND WALK HUMBLY WITH GOD.

Dear Lord,
Help me to deal justly with others.
Amen.

KINDNESS

A KIND PERSON is often hard to find. Relief pitcher Dave Righetti demonstrated kindness when he pitched for the New York Yankees. Neither his owner, George Steinbrenner, nor his manager, Billy Martin, were liked by many players. Yet, *Sports Illustrated* reported that Dave sent thank you notes of appreciation to Steinbrenner for his gifts honoring his great seasons. And Dave was one of the few Yankees to send flowers to Martin's funeral in 1989. While others forgot or ignored the occasion, Righetti remembered with kindness.

APPLICATION

KINDNESS IS IMPORTANT to the God who sees every deed and hears every word. It's an attitude we must not live without.

DEFINITIONS:

Ruthless — "Cruel."

CHARACTER CALISTHENICS:

How Are God's People to Behave Towards One Another?

Be _____ and _____ to one another, forgiving each other, just as in _____ God _____ you.

Ephesians 4:32

Therefore, as God's _____ people, _____ , and dearly _____ , clothe yourselves with

_____ , _____ , _____ , _____ , and _____ .

Colossians 3:12

What is Gained When We Are Kind?

A _____ woman gains _____ , but _____ men gain only wealth. A _____ man benefits _____ , but a _____ man brings _____ on himself.

Proverbs 11:16, 17

Who Will Reward Kindness?

He who is _____ to the _____
lends to the _____ , and he will _____   *Oppresses* " "Puts
him for what he has done.   down."
Proverbs 19:17

If your _____ is hungry, give him _____
to eat; if he is thirsty, give him _____ to
drink. In doing this, you will heap burning _____   *Contempt* — "Hatred."
on his head, and the _____ will reward you.
Proverbs 25:21,22

SHORT SPRINTS:

    1. To be kind to the needy honors God (Proverbs 14:31).   T   F
    2. God is not kind to the ungrateful and the wicked
        (Luke 6:35).   T   F
    3. Love is kind (1 Corinthians 13:4).   T   F

MIND STRETCHERS:

Who do you know who is kind?

How can you be more kind at home?

At school?

In sports?

STRENGTHEN YOUR GRIP:
Write out Proverbs 12:25:

_____

_____

_____

_____

| **Be Kind to One Another.** |

Dear Lord,
Help me to be kind to others.
Amen

KNOWLEDGE

JOE DiMAGGIO was a great centerfielder for the New York Yankees. But the Yankees' right fielder, Tommy Henrich, never played in the shadow of DiMaggio, even though he couldn't match Joe's skill. Henrich always seemed to know exactly what to do with the ball. He established a reputation for his great knowledge of the game. "Catching a fly ball is a pleasure," said Tommy. "But knowing what to do with it after you catch it is a business." No one knew his business like Tommy Henrich, whom Yankee fans nicknamed "Old Reliable."

APPLICATION

IF KNOWLEDGE of games and business is so important, how much more important is the knowledge of how to live? Let's see what the Proverbs say about gaining knowledge.

DEFINITIONS:

Knowledge — "Awareness of facts; understanding."

Fools — "Those with no desire to know God."

Mocker — "One who makes fun of God and Godly ideas."

Discerning — "One who sees truth."

Zeal — "Enthusiasm."

Hasty — "Acting too quickly."

CHARACTER CALISTHENICS:

What is the First Step in Gaining True Knowledge?

The _____ of the _____ is the _____ of _____ , but _____ despise _____ and _____ .

Proverbs 1:7

What Three Virtues Did God Demonstrate When He Created the Earth?

By _____ the Lord laid the _____ foundations, by _____ he set the _____ in place; by his _____ the deeps were divided and the clouds let drop the dew.

Proverbs 3:19, 20

Who Stores Up Knowledge?

_____ men store up _____ ,
but the mouth of a _____ invites ruin.

Proverbs 10:14

The _____ seeks _____ and
finds none, but _____ comes
easily to the _____ .

Proverbs 14:6

The _____ of the wise spread _____ ;
not so the hearts of _____ .

Proverbs 15:7

What Value is Knowledge?

With his mouth the _____ destroys his
neighbor, but through _____ the
righteous _____ .

Proverbs 11:9

It is not good to have _____ without
_____ , nor to be _____
and miss the way.

Proverbs 19:2

How Can You Identify a Man of Knowledge?

A man of _____ uses words with
_____ , and a man of understanding is
_____ .

Proverbs 17:27

SHORT SPRINTS:

    1. Fools hate knowledge (Proverbs 1:22).   T   F

    2. Knowledge comes from God (Proverbs 2:6).   T   F

    3. Whoever loves discipline loves knowledge
        (Proverbs 12:1).   T   F

MIND STRETCHERS:

Who is the most knowledgable person you know?

How can you gain more knowledge about how to live?

About the world around you?

About other people?

STRENGTHEN YOUR GRIP:

Write out Proverbs 24:5:

_____

_____

_____

_____

**A WISE MAN IS ALWAYS READY TO LISTEN
AND GAIN MORE KNOWLEDGE.**

Dear Lord,
*   Help me to listen to You for the knowledge*
I need.

*   Amen.*

LOVE

JOHNNY AND MARTY were boyhood friends in Atlanta who loved baseball and made a pact to always play together — no matter what happened. Johnny became the star of his team, while Marty was an "ugly duckling." One day their coach told Johnny about a minor league tryout.

"Marty and I will sign up right away," said Johnny. Both the coach and Johnny's mother tried to discourage including Marty, but Johnny stood by his friend. When Marty's mom asked Johnny why he was so determined to keep this pact, he replied, "Belief is a kind of love. I believe in Marty. We're friends. Believing in someone is the best kind of love."

Both players tried out. Johnny received a contract but Marty was cut. "Leave your buddy. You've got great natural talent and potential," said the minor league coach.

"It's both of us or neither of us," replied Johnny Echols. And he left. Such loyalty and love was rare, and several days later both boys were awarded contracts. Marty became deeply inspired and began to improve. During their third year in the minors, Johnny Echols quit. Marty was called up by the St. Louis Cardinals to play shortstop. He became the team leader of the dynasty known as the Gas House Gang of the 1940s. When they won the 1944 World Series, Marty Marion was named the Most Valuable player!

APPLICATION

REAL LOVE comes from the God who *is* love. Love has the power to believe in someone and to draw out the best in them. We must always be people who love.

DEFINITIONS:

Belief — "Commitment with action."

CHARACTER CALISTHENICS:

How Do We Know What Love Is?

This is how we know what _____ is: Jesus Christ _____ down his _____ for us. And we ought to _____ down our _____ for our _____ .

1 John 3:16

LOVE • 85

Dear children, let us not _____ with _____ or _____ but with _____ and in _____ .

1 John 3:18

For God so _____ the _____ that He _____ His _____ and only _____ , that whoever _____ in Him shall not _____ but have _____ life.

John 3:16

How Important is Love?

Let _____ and _____ never leave you; _____ them around your _____ , write them on the _____ of your _____ .

Proverbs 3:3

Better a meal of _____ where there is _____ than a _____ calf with _____ .

Proverbs 15:17

_____ and _____ keep a king safe; through _____ his throne is made _____ .

Proverbs 20:28

What are Characteristics of Love?

He who covers over an _____ promotes _____ , but whoever _____ the matter _____ close _____ .

Proverbs 17:9

A _____ loves at all _____ , and a _____ is born for _____ .

Proverbs 17:17

What is the Result of Loving Others?

He who pursues _____ and _____ finds _____ , _____ , and _____ .

Proverbs 21:21

Perish — "To be eternally separated from God."

Faithfulness — "Loyalty."

Adversity — "Hard times."

Righteousness — "Right standing with God."

SHORT SPRINTS:

    1. Deep down, we desire unfailing love (Proverbs 19:22).   T   F

    2. Love covers over wrongs done to us (Proverbs 10:12).   T   F

    3. Open rebuke is better than hidden love (Proverbs 27:5).   T   F

MIND STRETCHERS:

Who is the best example of one who loves others?

How do you demonstrate love in your family?

At school?

In sports?

STRENGTHEN YOUR GRIP:

Write out 1 John 4:7, 8:

_____

_____

_____

_____

LOVE COMES FROM GOD.
WHEN WE LOVE OTHERS BY OUR DEEDS
WE ARE REVEALING THAT WE KNOW HIM.

Dear Lord,
    Help me to really love others.
                Amen.

PATIENCE

AN OLD MAXIM SAYS, "Success comes to those who wait." If we study the careers of famous athletes, we see that many have struggled through hard times before reaching great heights. Success seems to have been mixed with liberal doses of failure along the way for Babe Ruth, who hit 714 career home runs but struck out 1330 times. How about Ty Cobb, who stole 96 bases one year but was thrown out 38 times in the same season. Or Cy Young, who won 511 games but also lost 315. Or Reggie Jackson, recently named to the Hall of Fame. Reggie hit a ton of home runs, but was the first major leaguer to strike out 2000 times in a career!

These men all had the patience to wait for success. They were not afraid to fail along the way.

APPLICATION

MANY PROVERBS explain how a patient man would respond to certain situations. Let's examine several responses of a patient person.

DEFINITIONS:

Folly — "Foolishness."

Dissension — "Arguments."

Wisdom — "Insight into problems."

CHARACTER CALISTHENICS:

How does a Patient Man Differ from a Hot-Tempered Man?

A _____ man has great _____ but a _____ man displays

_____ .

Proverbs 14:29

A _____ man stirs up _____ , but a _____ man

_____ a quarrel.

Proverbs 15:18

A man's _____ gives him _____ ; it is to his _____ to overlook an offense.

Proverbs 19:11

Who Will Repay Evil Deeds?

Do not say, "I'll pay you back for this wrong!"
_____ for the _____ , and he will
_____ _____ .

Proverbs 20:22

Be still before the _____ and wait _____
for _____ .

Psalm 37:7

Be _____ , then, brothers, until the
Lord's _____ .

James 5:7

SHORT SPRINTS:

1. Abraham received God's promises of blessing and descendants
   because he waited on God (Hebrews 6:15).   T   F
2. Christians are to be patient with everybody
   (1 Thessalonians 5:14).   T   F
3. Job and other prophets of God are poor examples
   of patience (James 5:10, 11).   T   F

MIND STRETCHERS:

Who is the most patient person you know?

In what circumstances do you need more patience?

STRENGTHEN YOUR GRIP:

Write out Proverbs 16:32:

_____

_____

_____

_____

```
WAIT ON THE LORD
AND
HE WILL DELIVER YOU.
```

Dear Lord,
   Help me to be patient whenever I must wait.
                                    Amen.

PEACEFUL

INNER PEACE AND CONTENTMENT is a futile pursuit for many people in American society. Until we find peace with God and with ourselves, we will never enjoy life, achieve our potential, or find peace with others. Former Seattle Seahawk punter Rick Donneley had this to say about peace with God and life in the NFL: "The NFL is a pressure cooker, especially for place kickers and punters. Before Christ, I had always felt as if I had no one to turn to with my concerns and dilemmas. God has taught me to give my football career to Him, in the down times and the glory times. The game is important because anything we do as Christians is important to God. It is still only part of life, however, not life itself."

APPLICATION

IT IS THE PEACE OF GOD that enables a punter like Rick Donneley to relax and kick his best. That inner peace from God is available to all believers in spite of the turmoil in the world.

DEFINITIONS:

Strife — "Conflict."

Deceit — "Cruel trickery."

Envy — "To hate the success of someone else."

CHARACTER CALISTHENICS:

What Value does God Place Upon Peace in the Home?
Better a dry _____ with _____ and _____ than a house full of _____ with _____ .

Proverbs 17:1

How is Peace Related to Honor?
It is to a man's _____ to avoid _____ , but every _____ is quick to _____ .

Proverbs 20:3

What are some Benefits of Promoting Peace?
There is _____ in the hearts of those who plot _____ , but _____ for those who promote _____ .

Proverbs 12:20

A heart at peace gives _____ to the body,
but _____ rots the bones.

Proverbs 14:30

Justified — "Counted righteous by God."

How do We Obtain Peace with God?
Therefore, since we have been _____
through faith, we have _____ with God
through our Lord _____ _____ .

Romans 5:1

SHORT SPRINTS:
1. There is a future for the man of peace (Psalm 37:37).   T   F
2. My pleasing the Lord has no effect upon my enemies
   (Proverbs 16:7).   T   F
3. Peace comes when Jesus comes (Isaiah 9:6, 7).   T   F

MIND STRETCHERS:
Who do you know who most often demonstrates the peace of God?

Are you experiencing God's peace in your heart?

STRENGTHEN YOUR GRIP:
Write out Psalm 119:165:

_____

_____

_____

_____

94 • PEACEFUL

> ## WE MUST EXPERIENCE PEACE *WITH* GOD
> ## BEFORE WE CAN KNOW THE PEACE *OF* GOD.

Dear Lord,
ThankYou for the peace that passes my understanding.
Amen.

PRAYERFUL

NAT "SWEETWATER" CLIFTON was a star basketball player with the New York Knicks and the Detroit Pistons during the 1950s. Clifton, who got his nickname because he preferred a 7-up or Coke over beer and liquor, had once played for the Harlem Globetrotters. He played before the salary explosion in pro sports and did his own negotiating. In all his years of playing, Nat never made more than $10,000 a year.

Looking back over his career, Nat regrets that he never made more money. Yet, he doesn't hold it against the owners.

"The guys I negotiated with . . . were nice guys,' he said. "They gave me whatever I asked for. I just didn't ask for enough."

APPLICATION

SOMETIMES, CHRISTIANS are guilty of not asking God for enough. We settle for second best when we could be enjoying the fullness of His Spirit in every part of our lives. God tells us we are always to be asking, seeking, and knocking on His door in prayer.

DEFINITIONS:

Detests — "Hates."

Saints — "People who have trusted Christ as their personal Savior and Lord."

CHARACTER CALISTHENICS:

Whose Prayers Does God Hear?

The Lord is far from the _____ but he _____ the prayer of the _____ .

Proverbs 15:29

The Lord _____ the sacrifice of the _____ , but the prayer of the _____ pleases him.

Proverbs 15:8

How Often Should We Pray?

Pray _____ .

1 Thessalonians 5:17

And pray in the _____ on all _____ with all kinds of prayers and _____ . With this in _____ , be _____ and always keep on praying for all the _____ .

Ephesians 6:18

How Should We Pray?

This, then, is how you should pray: "Our _____ in _____ , _____ be your _____ , your _____ come, your _____ be done on earth as it is in _____ . Give us today our daily _____ . _____ us our debts, as we also have _____ our debtors. And _____ us not into _____ , but _____ us from the _____ one."

Matthew 6:9-13

Hallowed — "Honored, respected, reverenced."

Debts — "That which we owe to another."

Debtors — "Those who owe us."

SHORT SPRINTS:

1. God detests the prayers of those who ignore the law (Proverbs 28:9). T F
2. We are to pray for those who mistreat us (Matthew 5:44). T F
3. Believing prayer makes a difference (Mark 11:24). T F

MIND STRETCHERS:

Who is the most prayerful person you know?

How has prayer helped you?

What prayers has God answered?

What prayers are you still waiting for God to answer?

STRENGTHEN YOUR GRIP:

Write out Luke 18:1:

_____

_____

_____

_____

> ## GOD HEARS
> ### AND
> ## ANSWERS
> # PRAYER.

Dear Lord,
> *Give me strength to keep praying
and not to give up.*
>> *Amen.*

PROSPERITY

LIKE MOST SUPERSTARS, Julius Erving (Dr. J.) is often asked about the greatest highlight or most outstanding performance of his illustrious career. Though Dr. J. enjoyed one of the greatest careers in NBA history, he likes to share what went on in his heart.

"At age 29 I realized I was looking good on the outside, but was hitting a lot of peaks and valleys on the inside." He says, "After searching for the meaning of life for over ten years, I found the meaning in Jesus Christ."

"When I gave my life to Jesus Christ, I began to understand my true purpose for being here. It's not to go through life and experience as many things as you possibly can and then turn to dust and be no more. The purpose of life is to be found through having Christ in your life, and understanding what His plan is, and following that plan."

Surely, God prospered Dr. J. in basketball and in the game of life!

APPLICATION

GOD WANTS THINGS to go well for us. Scripture tells us repeatedly that He desires good and not evil, prosperity and not poverty, peace and not war for His people. Sometimes (not always) when we suffer it is because we have turned away from Him in our heart and He is trying to get our attention. He does not like our independence, but wants us to realize we are dependent upon Him. While real prosperity is more a condition of our hearts and He does not promise us fancy clothes and expensive cars, God does promise to bless us with food, clothing, and shelter as we seek Him (Matthew 6).

DEFINITIONS:

Prosperity — "Success both spiritually and physically."

CHARACTER CALISTHENICS:

What is the Connection between Righteousness and Prosperity?

_____ pursues the _____ ,
but _____ is the _____
of the _____ .

Proverbs 13:21

The _____ eat to their heart's content,
but the _____ of the wicked goes
_____ .

Proverbs 13:25

The _____ of the _____ is their crown, but the _____ of fools yields _____ .

Proverbs 14:24

The house of the _____ contains great _____ , but the _____ of the _____ brings them _____ .

Proverbs 15:6

A _____ man will be richly _____ , but one eager to get _____ will not go unpunished.

Proverbs 28:20

What are God's Principles of Handling Wealth?

He who loves _____ will become _____ : whoever loves _____ and _____ will never be _____ .

The _____ become a ransom for the _____ and the _____ for the _____ .

Proverbs 21:17, 18

In the house of the _____ are stores of choice _____ and _____ , but a _____ man devours all he has.

Proverbs 21:20

The _____ rule over the _____ and the _____ is servant to the _____ .

Proverbs 22:7

Do not wear yourself out to get _____ ; have the _____ to show restraint. Cast but a glance at _____ and they are gone, for they will surely sprout wings and fly off to the sky like an eagle.

Proverbs 23:4, 5

Folly — "Foolish waste."

Fools — "Unwise people."

Security — "Money given to insure someone else's promises."

Devours — "Wastefully consumes."

SHORT SPRINTS:
1. It is best to earn money little by little to make it grow
   (Proverbs 13:11).   T   F
2. We should not provide "security" for someone else's
   promises (Proverbs 17:18).   T   F
3. There is no blessing of God on a faithful man
   (Proverbs 28:20).   T   F

MIND STRETCHERS:
How has God prospered you?

What does He want you to do with what He has given?

STRENGTHEN YOUR GRIP:
Write out Jeremiah 29:11:

_____

_____

_____

_____

**GOD WANTS TO BLESS US TO THE POINT
THAT WE WILL KEEP OUR EYES ONLY ON HIM
AND NOT UPON WHAT HE GIVES US.**

Dear Lord,
   Bless my life to the degree that is best.
                          Amen.

PRUDENCE

BEFORE THE 1986 SEASON, Cincinnati Reds outfielder Eric Davis heard excessive praise and high expectations coming from former great Willie Mays, manager Roger Craig, and others. Eric responded with prudence and insight. "I don't try to live up to anybody's expectations. You can't play that way. I've heard nice things about me before . . . all of us have to learn. Even when you're a success everything is a learning process."

APPLICATION

SOMETIMES, PRAISE and the expectations of others can become a real trial. Eric Davis demonstrated a prudent attitude when he received much praise. Let's look at God's Word concerning prudent attitudes and behavior.

DEFINITIONS:

Prudence — "Sensible, sound judgment in practical matters."

Discretion — "Sound judgment."

Folly — "Silliness."

CHARACTER CALISTHENICS:

What are the Simple Told to Obtain?

You who are simple, gain _____ : you who are foolish, gain _____ .

Proverbs 8:5

What other Traits are Closely Associated with Prudence?

I, _____ , dwell together with prudence; I possess _____ and _____ .

Proverbs 8:12

What are some Characteristics of a Prudent Man or Woman?

A _____ man keeps his _____ to himself, but the heart of _____ blurts out

_____ .

Proverbs 12:23

Every _____ man acts out of _____ , but a _____ exposes his _____ .

Proverbs 13:16

PRUDENCE • 105

The _____ of the prudent is to give
_____ to their ways, but the
_____ of fools is _____ .
                                    Proverbs 14:8
A _____ spurns his father's _____ ,
but whoever heeds _____ shows
_____ .
                                    Proverbs 15:5

SHORT SPRINTS:
1. A prudent wife comes from God (Proverbs 19:14).   T   F
2. It is not prudent to overlook an insult (Proverbs 12:16).   T   F
3. A prudent man gives no thought to his step
   (Proverbs 14:15).   T   F

MIND STRETCHERS:
Who is the most prudent person you know?

How does prudence help you?

STRENGTHEN YOUR GRIP:
Write out Proverbs 22:3:

_____

_____

_____

_____

> ## PRUDENT BEHAVIOR WILL SAVE YOU FROM MUCH TROUBLE.

Dear Lord,
> *Help me to think and act with prudence.*
> > *Amen.*

PURE SPEECH

THE WORDS WE USE to communicate have great power to build up or to tear down. Steve Alford, a Christian young person in college, had this to say about the difficulty of playing for a coach who paid no attention to how he expressed himself:

"The worst part of it, for me, was the profanity. I knew all the words — I hadn't led that sheltered a life — but I had never heard them in such abundance and with so much fury behind them. To a young man of my background and religious beliefs, coach's vulgarity was like a punch in the stomach."

APPLICATION

LET'S EXAMINE what God says in Proverbs concerning pure speech.

DEFINITIONS:

Nourish — "Feed."

Perverse — "Vile, corrupt."

CHARACTER CALISTHENICS:

How do the Words of a Wise, Righteous Man Differ from those of a Wicked, Foolish Man?

The mouth of the _____ brings forth _____ , but a _____ tongue will be cut out. The lips of the _____ know what is _____ , but the mouth of the _____ only what is _____ .

Proverbs 10:31, 32

The _____ of the _____ lie in wait for _____ , but the _____ of the _____ rescues them.

Proverbs 12:6

An _____ man is trapped by his sinful _____ , but a _____ man escapes _____ .

Proverbs 12:13

A fool's _____ brings a rod to his _____ , but the lips of the _____ protect them.

Proverbs 14:3

PURE SPEECH • 109

The tongue of the _____ commends
_____ , but the mouth of the
_____ gushes _____ .

Proverbs 15:2

Commends — "Praises."

A _____ man's _____ guides
his _____ , and his lips _____
instruction.

Proverbs 16:23

Judgment — "Discretion."

How Should We Be Using Our Mouths?

A man who lacks _____ derides his
neighbor, but a man of _____ holds
his _____ .

Proverbs 11:12

Derides — "Talks down about."

He who _____ his lips guards his _____ ,
but he who speaks _____ will come to
_____ .

Proverbs 13:3

Calamity — "Disaster."

The heart of the _____ weighs its
answers, but the mouth of the _____ gushes
_____ .

Proverbs 15:28

SHORT SPRINTS:

1. The more we talk, the more likely we are to sin
   (Proverbs 10:19).   T   F
2. Fools die for lack of judgment (Proverbs 10:21).   T   F
3. It doesn't matter what you say (Proverbs 21:23).   T   F

MIND STRETCHERS:

Who always seems to speak wisely?

How can you remember to use kind words?

STRENGTHEN YOUR GRIP:
    Write out Proverbs 12:18:

_____

_____

_____

_____

> ## HE WHO GUARDS HIS LIPS
> ## GUARDS HIS LIFE.

Dear Lord,
    Help me to keep my mouth from talking
trash.
                        Amen.

MORE PURE SPEECH

CARELESS WORDS have been known to get more than one man in deep trouble. On September 29, 1985, they got Baltimore Oriole's manager Earl Weaver in trouble twice! Weaver was ejected from the first game of a doubleheader when he charged out of the dugout to argue with the umpires for the third time. Then, while delivering the lineup card at the start of game two, his ill-timed criticism got him thrown out again — before the game even started!

APPLICATION

JUST AS PLEASANT words have positive effects upon the hearer, gossip and deceit have a negative effect. Let's examine the differences.

DEFINITIONS:

CHARACTER CALISTHENICS:

What is the Effect of Pleasant Words?

A _____ answer turns away _____ ,
but a _____ word stirs up _____ .
                                                    Proverbs 15:1

Apt — "Helpful."

A man finds _____ in giving an _____
reply — and how good is a timely _____ !
                                                    Proverbs 15:23

Pleasant words are a _____ , sweet
to the _____ and _____ to the
bones.
                                                    Proverbs 16:24

Gossip — "Talking about others with no helpful intention."

From the _____ of his mouth a man's
_____ is filled; with the _____
from his lips he is _____ .
                                                    Proverbs 18:20

What is the Effect of Gossip and Deceit?

A _____ betrays a _____ , but a
_____ man keeps a _____ .
                                                    Proverbs 11:13

A _____ man stirs up _____ ,
and a _____ separates _____
friends .

Betray — "To be disloyal while pretending to be loyal."

Proverbs 16:28

A man of _____ heart does not _____ ;
he whose _____ is _____ falls
into trouble.

Confidence — "Personal trust."

Proverbs 17:20

Perverse — "Evil."

A fool's _____ is his undoing, and his lips
are a _____ to his soul. The words of a
_____ are like choice _____ ;
they go down to a man's _____ parts.

Dissention — "Arguments."

Proverbs 18:7, 8

Morsels — "Small bits of food."

SHORT SPRINTS:

    1. A lying tongue lasts forever (Proverbs 12:19).   T   F
    2. A fool's mouth invites a beating (Proverbs 18:6).   T   F
    3. Without gossip a quarrel dies down (Proverbs 26:20).   T   F

MIND STRETCHERS:

Who do you know who always seems to use pure speech?

How can you improve your speech at home?

At school?

In your sport?

STRENGTHEN YOUR GRIP:
    Write out Proverbs 15:4:

_____

_____

_____

_____

**THE TONGUE HAS THE POWER
OF LIFE AND DEATH,
SO BE CAREFUL HOW YOU USE IT.**

Dear Lord,
    Help me to speak pleasant words
at just the right time.
                    Amen.

PURITY

REGGIE JACKSON was a star outfielder with the New York Yankees. In 1980, Reggie somehow misplaced his 1978 World Series ring. The ring was found by Virginia Overholtz in a small pile of rubbish in an auto refurbishing plant in Scranton, Pennsylvania. Did Virginia keep the expensive ring or try to sell it for a profit? No. She did the only right and pure thing she could do. Virginia contacted the Yankees and returned the ring to Reggie!

APPLICATION

MANY PEOPLE today are not pure in heart and do not act in purity. Let's see what God says about purity.

DEFINITIONS:

Purity — "Moral excellence."

Detests — "Hates."

CHARACTER CALISTHENICS:

What Kinds of Thoughts Please God?

The Lord _____ the thoughts of the _____ , but those of the _____ are _____ to him.

Proverbs 15:26

Finally, brothers, whatever is _____ , whatever is _____ , whatever is _____ , whatever is _____ , whatever is _____ , whatever is _____ — if anything is _____ or _____ — think about such things.

Philippians 4:8

How are We to Keep Ourselves?

. . . keep yourself _____ .

1 Timothy 5:22

Everyone who has this hope (being like Jesus) in him _____ himself, just as he is _____ .

1 John 3:3

What are some Rewards of a Pure Heart?

He who loves a _____ heart and whose _____
is _____ will have the _____
for his friend.

Gracious — "Full of grace."

Proverbs 22:11

Blessed are the _____ in heart, for they will
see _____ .

Matthew 5:8

SHORT SPRINTS:

1. No one is totally without sin (Proverbs 20:9).   T   F
2. Those pure in their own eyes are not necessarily clean
   (Proverbs 30:12).   T   F
3. To the pure, all things are pure (Titus 1:15).   T   F

MIND STRETCHERS:

How have you chosen purity over moral filth at school?

In sports?

On TV?

STRENGTHEN YOUR GRIP:

Write out Proverbs 20:11

_____

_____

_____

_____

> ## GOD'S CHILDREN
> ## MUST LIVE LIVES
> ## THAT ARE PURE.

Dear Lord,
    Purify my thoughts, words, and actions.
                    Amen.

RIGHTEOUSNESS

TIM BURKE was an outstanding pitcher in high school. He has always "believed" in God and attended church regularly with his parents . . . until he went to college. From the first day he arrived at the University of Nebraska on a full scholarship, Tim ran with the wrong crowd. He was constantly in trouble.

"I worked real hard during baseball practice. Then when I went back to the dorm, I worked real hard going to parties and developing a terrible drinking habit. It wasn't until my junior year in college that I realized how stupid I was."

Still, Tim was All-Big-Eight three years in a row. When he signed a professional contract, baseball became a job and a god to him. After two weeks of marriage, his wife was ready to leave him. Then Tim's teammates got him and Christine to attend a Bible study.

"At the Bible study I realized I needed to invite Jesus Christ into my life and let Him take control instead of me trying to run things," he says. "I knew if I had kept on going like I was, I was headed for real trouble. Christine and I both gave our lives to Jesus Christ and we began to live a new and beautiful life together.

APPLICATION

WHEN TIM gave his life to Jesus, his lifestyle changed. Unrighteous deeds were replaced by the righteousness of Christ. He was counted righteous in God's eyes. Old things passed away. All things became new.

DEFINITIONS:

Righteousness — "Right standing with God which results in Godly living."

CHARACTER CALISTHENICS:

Of What Value is Righteousness?

Ill-gotten _____ are of no _____, but _____ delivers from _____ .

Proverbs 10:2

The _____ of the blameless makes a _____ way for them, but the _____ are brought down by their own _____ . The _____ of the upright _____ them, but the _____ are _____ by evil desires.

Proverbs 11:5, 6

The _____ man is _____ from
trouble, and it comes on the _____ instead.
Proverbs 11:8

The name of the _____ is a strong tower;
the _____ run to it and are _____ .
Proverbs 18:10

How does the Final Outcome of the Righteous Differ from the Final Outcome of the Wicked?

The prospect of the _____ is _____ ,
but the hopes of the _____ come to
_____ .
Proverbs 10:28

Be sure of this: The _____ will not go
_____ , but those who are _____
will go _____ .
Proverbs 11:21

Perverse — "Grossly evil."

What the _____ dreads will overtake
him; what the _____ desire will be
_____ .
Proverbs 10:24

The _____ will never be _____ ,
but the _____ will not remain in the
_____ .
Proverbs 10:30

What Traits do Righteous People Possess?

The _____ of the _____ brings
forth _____ , but a _____ tongue
will be cut out. The lips of the _____
know what is fitting, but the mouth of the wicked
only what is _____ .
Proverbs 10:31, 32

The lips of the _____ nourish many,
but _____ die for lack of _____ .
Proverbs 10:21

A _____ man cares for the needs
of his _____ , but the kindest acts of the
_____ are cruel.
Proverbs 12:10

SHORT SPRINTS:

    1. God hates the way of the wicked and loves those who pursue
        righteousness. (Proverbs 15:8, 9).   T   F
    2. A king remains in power through wickedness
        (Proverbs 16:12).   T   F
    3. The "good guys" (righteous) win in the end
        (Proverbs 11:19).   T   F

MIND STRETCHERS:

Who do you think of when you hear the word "righteous?"

What does righteous conduct mean to you?

STRENGTHEN YOUR GRIP:

Write out Proverbs 14:34:

_____

_____

_____

_____

RIGHTEOUSNESS RESULTS IN LIFE AND WICKEDNESS RESULTS IN DEATH.

Dear Lord,

    Help me to seek your righteousness every day of my life.

                       Amen.

SELF-CONTROL

ON AUGUST 28, 1956, Sammy White payed the price of a temper tantrum. The Red Sox catcher got so upset while arguing a play at home plate, he heaved the ball into center field — forgetting that it was still in play! Sammy was horrified to watch the Tigers' Red Wilson scamper from first base all the way around to score! Because of his frustration and his temper, Sammy White had cost his team a run that should not have scored.

APPLICATION

GOD'S PEOPLE are to be people of self-control. Whenever we lose control, we risk hurting ourselves as well as others.

DEFINITIONS:

Zeal – "Enthusiasm."

Hasty — "To move too fast."

Ensnared — "Trapped."

Vent — "Release."

CHARACTER CALISTHENICS:

To What is a Man Who Lacks Self-Control Compared?

Like a _____ whose walls are _____ down is a _____ who lacks _____ - _____ .

Proverbs 25:28

What Traits come from God's Spirit?

For God did not give us a spirit of _____ , but a spirit of _____ , of _____ and of _____ - _____ .

2 Timothy 1:7

What Difference Does Self-Control Make in a Person's Life?

It is not good to have_____ without _____ , nor to be _____ and miss the way.

Proverbs 19:2

Do not make friends with a _____ man, do not _____ with one easily _____ , or you may learn his ways and get yourself _____ .

Proverbs 22:24, 25

SHORT SPRINTS:

     1. It is better to be a patient person than a powerful warrior
        (Proverbs 16:32).   T   F

     2. A wise man gives full vent to his anger (Proverbs 29:11).   T   F

     3. A fool keeps himself under control (Proverbs 29:11).   T   F

MIND STRETCHERS:

     Name a person who has great self-control.

     How does it help him/her?

STRENGTHEN YOUR GRIP:

     Write out Galatians 5:22-23:

SELF-CONTROL KEEPS US OUT OF MUCH TROUBLE.

Dear Lord,
    Help me to live with self-discipline.
                                    Amen.

TEACHABILITY

LEARNING TO BE an outstanding ballplayer requires certain attributes as well as certain actions. First, a player must realize his current level of skill and where he needs to improve. This requires humility. Secondly, a young player must be provided with good information from coaches who know the sport. Finally, the player must apply self-discipline and dedication to excel. This requires perseverence in practice.

If a player refuses instruction, there is little hope for improvement. That's why the character trait of teachability is so vital.

APPLICATION

NONE OF US KNOWS everything about anything. Therefore, we must remain teachable throughout our lives. God has much to say about our continued learning.

DEFINITIONS:

Instruction — "Direction."

Mocker — "One who pokes fun at someone or something."

Folly — "Foolishness."

Shame — "Disgrace."

Contemptuous — "Disregarding in anger."

CHARACTER CALISTHENICS:

What Should Be our Attitude toward Wise Instruction?

_____ , my sons, to a father's _____ ;
pay attention and gain _____ .

Proverbs 4:1

A wise son _____ his father's _____ ,
but a _____ does not _____ to rebuke.

Proverbs 13:1

He who _____ before _____ —
that is his _____ and his _____ .

Proverbs 18:13

After Hearing Instruction, What Must We Do with It?

_____ on to _____ , do not let it
go; _____ it well, for it is your life.

Proverbs 4:13

He who _____ instructions _____
his life, but he who is _____ of his
ways will _____ .

Proverbs 19:16

What are the Results of Listening to Instructions?

Whoever gives _____ to instruction _____ , and _____ is he who _____ in the Lord.

Proverbs 16:20

Prospers — "Has enough."

He who obeys _____ guards his life, but he who is _____ of his ways will _____ .

Proverbs 19:16

Discerning — "Able to distinguish truth."

SHORT SPRINTS:

1. Once we are "in the know" we can stop listening (Proverbs 19:27).   T   F
2. A wise man makes the best instructor (Proverbs 16:23).   T   F
3. Harsh words promote instruction (Proverbs 16:21).   T   F

MIND STRETCHERS:

Who is the best teacher you know?

Why is he or she a good teacher?

STRENGTHEN YOUR GRIP:

Write out Proverbs 19:20:

_____

_____

_____

_____

BECAUSE NONE OF US KNOWS EVERYTHING ABOUT ANYTHING, WE MUST REMAIN TEACHABLE THROUGHOUT LIFE.

Dear Lord,

      Help me to listen to wise words of instruction.

                                  Amen.

THANKFULNESS

THE BOSTON COLLEGE EAGLES had a reason to be thankful for a stunning 1942 upset by the Holy Cross. BC was the number one football team in the nation with a perfect 8-0 record. They had shut out five opponents and outscored teams 249-19 before facing the 4-4-1 Crusaders. Skillful coaching and tremendous incentive led Holy Cross to a 55-12 upset in the fierce intrastate rivalry. The cocky Eagles canceled a planned celebration at the Coconut Grove, one of Boston's fanciest nightspots.

That night, with the nightclub jammed beyond capacity with about 1000 patrons, a 15-minute fire broke out killing 491 people in the second deadliest fire in American history. Because they had lost and canceled their party, the Boston College players were safe at home.

APPLICATION

IT WOULD BE EASY to thank God for a loss that saved your life. But God expects His people to be thankful in all circumstances, for only He can see the end from the beginning.

DEFINITIONS:

CHARACTER CALISTHENICS:

Circumstances — "Whatever happens."

What is to be Our Attitude in All Circumstances?

Let the _____ of Christ rule in your _____ , since as members of one body you were called to _____ . And be _____ .

Colossians 3:15

Always giving _____ to _____ the Father for _____ , in the name of our Lord _____ _____ .

Ephesians 5:20

Give _____ in all _____ , for this is God's_____ for you in _____ _____ .

1 Thessalonians 5:18

Do not be _____ about _____ , but in _____ , by _____ and _____ , with _____ , present your _____ to God.

Philippians 4:6

Let us come before Him with _____ and extol Him with _____ and _____ .

Petition —"Thoughtful request."

Psalm 95:2

Enter his gates with _____ and his courts with _____ ; give _____ to Him and _____ his name.

Psalm 100:4

Sing to the Lord with _____ ; make music to our God on the harp.

Extol — "To speak of the fine qualities of someone or something."

Psalm 147:7

SHORT SPRINTS:

1. Praise and thanks to God pleases Him more than the sacrifice of animals (Psalm 69:30, 31).　　　　T　　　F

2. Being unthankful leads to sin in other area (Romans 1:21).　　　　T　　　F

3. Jesus remembered to give thanks to God for food (John 6:11).　　　　T　　　F

MIND STRETCHERS:

Who do you think of when you hear the word "thankful?"

What are you most thankful for at home?

At school?

In your sport?

STRENGTHEN YOUR GRIP:
Write out 1 Corinthians 15:57:

_____

_____

_____

_____

> ## AN ATTITUDE
> ## OF GRATITUDE
> ## PLEASES GOD.

Dear Lord,
Thank you for everything you are doing in my life.
Amen.

UNDERSTANDING

JIM PALMER was a dominant pitcher during the 1970s. He had a great deal of understanding about the game of baseball, realizing just what it took to win. Palmer said, "You must accept that you'll give up runs. The pitcher who gives up runs one at a time wins, while the pitcher who gives them up two, three, and four at a time loses. I've given up long home runs that I turned around and admired like a fan. But the ones I admired were all solos." In almost 4,000 innings pitched, Jim Palmer never gave up a grand slam!

APPLICATION

IF WE HAD as much understanding about life as Jim Palmer had about pitching, things would go much easier for us. Let's see what the Proverbs tell us about understanding.

DEFINITIONS:

Understanding — "Insight or discernment."

Insight — "Ability to see inside a problem."

Folly — "Foolishness."

Fools — "Those who practice folly."

Soul — "The real you."

CHARACTER CALISTHENICS:

Who is the Source of Understanding?
For the _____ gives wisdom, and from his _____ come _____ and
_____ .

Proverbs 2:6

What Does Understanding Do for Us?
Discretion will _____ you, and _____ will _____ you.

Proverbs 2:11

Good _____ wins _____ , but the way of the _____ is _____ .

Proverbs 13:15

He who gets _____ loves his own soul; he who cherishes _____ prospers.

Proverbs 19:8

How does a Man of Understanding Act?

A _____ finds pleasure in _____
conduct, but a man of _____
delights in _____ .

Proverbs 10:23

Folly delights a man who lacks _____ ,
but a man of _____ keeps a
_____ course.

Proverbs 15:21

A man of _____ uses words
with _____ , and a man of _____
is even-tempered.

Proverbs 17:27

SHORT SPRINTS:

1. Understanding brings punishment (Proverbs 16:22).   T   F
2. It takes work to gain understanding (Proverbs 2:1-5).   T   F
3. Understanding is gained by listening to a wise father
   (Proverbs 4:1).   T   F

MIND STRETCHERS:

Who do you know who seems to have good understanding?

How is understanding demonstrated?

STRENGTHEN YOUR GRIP:
Write out Proverbs 3:19:

_____

_____

_____

_____

> ## GOOD UNDERSTANDING SAVES US FROM MUCH TROUBLE.

Dear Lord,
Help me to study to acquire greater understanding.
Amen.

WISDOM

BROOKLYN DODGER manager Walter Alston made a very wise move in the sixth inning of game seven of the 1955 World Series against the New York Yankees. Leading 2-0, he inserted the fleet Sandy Amoros in left field to replace a slower Junior Gilliam. With two on in the bottom of the sixth, Yogi Berra (normally a left-handed pull hitter) hit a fly ball directly down the left field line. The crowd, the third base coach, and both runners all thought it was a sure hit. But Amoros started running, caught the ball in full stride, and threw the ball to the infield to complete a double-play! The Yankees never threatened again and the Dodgers won the Series, 4 games to 3!

APPLICATION

THE WISDOM GOD gives includes the ability to put the right player into the game at the right time. But it also extends beyond baseball. To be really wise is to live with moral integrity and in right relationship to God.

DEFINITIONS:

Wisdom — "the ability to use knowledge in living a Godly life."

Knowledge — "aware-ness of facts."

CHARACTER CALISTHENICS:

How Valuable is Wisdom?

For _____ is more _____ than rubies, and nothing you _____ can compare with her.

Proverbs 8:11

What is the Source of Wisdom?

For the _____ gives wisdom, and from _____ mouth come _____ and _____ .

Proverbs 2:6

The rod of _____ imparts wisdom. But a child left to himself _____ his mother.

Proverbs 29:15

Of What Use is Wisdom?

_____ will save you from the _____ of _____ men, from men whose _____ are perverse.

Proverbs 2:12

_____ is the man who finds _____ , the man who gains _____ , for she is more _____ than _____ and yields better returns than _____ .

Proverbs 3:13

By _____ a house is built, and through _____ it is established.

Proverbs 24:3

What Accompanies Wisdom?

I, wisdom, dwell together with _____ , I possess _____ and _____ .

Proverbs 8:12

_____ and sound _____ are mine; I have _____ and _____ .

Proverbs 8:14

With me are _____ and _____ , enduring _____ and _____ .

Proverbs 8:18

Understanding — "insight or discern-ment."

Counsel — "wise advice."

Judgment — "good sense."

Wealth — "much money or property."

Prosperity — "things going well physically and spiritually."

SHORT SPRINTS:

1. Wisdom protects us if we do not forsake her (Proverbs 4:6).   T   F
2. I (wisdom) hate pride and arrogance (Proverbs 8:13).   T   F
3. He who trusts himself is a wise man (Proverbs 28:26).   T   F

MIND STRETCHERS:

Who do you know who is unusually wise?

How can you apply wisdom at home?

At school?

In your sport?

STRENGTHEN YOUR GRIP:
Write out Proverbs 4:6:

_____

_____

_____

_____

WISDOM (JESUS) INVITES YOU TO COME TO HIM
FOR UNDERSTANDING, KNOWLEDGE AND INSIGHT.

Dear Lord,
Give me wisdom to make wise decisions.
Amen.

THE WINNING RUN

In baseball, a runner must touch all four bases to score a run for his team. The path to abundant and eternal life is very similar to the base paths on a ball diamond.

Step 1 (first base) along that path is realizing that God created you. He knows you well, and loves you very much.

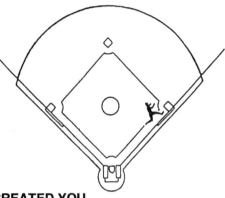

DEFINITIONS:

Create — "To cause to come into existance."

Perceive — "To grasp mentally."

Discern — "To recognize or perceive."

Perish — "To be utterly destroyed."

GOD CREATED YOU.

So God _____ man in his own _____ , in the image of _____ He created him; _____ and _____ He created them.

Genesis 1:27

For you _____ my inmost _____ ; you _____ me together in my mother's womb.

Psalm 139:13

GOD KNOWS YOU WELL.

You _____ when I _____ and when I _____ ; you _____ my thoughts from _____ . You _____ my going out and my lying down; you are _____ with all my _____ . Before a _____ is on my _____ you _____ it completely, O Lord.

Psalm 139:2-4

GOD LOVES YOU.

For God so loved (write your name here)

_____ (the world) that He _____ His one and only _____ , that whoever _____ in Him shall not _____ but have eternal _____ .

John 3:16

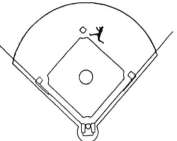

At second base (Step 2) you must admit you are a sinner, separated from fellowship with God and headed for an eternity of punishment apart from Him.

DEFINITIONS:

Fellowship — "Companionship."

Eternity — "Forever; without an end."

Iniquities — "Wicked, sinful acts."

Sins — "Violations of God's laws."

Tithes — "One-tenth of one's income."

Wages — "Payment for deeds done."

YOU ARE A SINNER.

For all (including: write your name

_____) have sinned and fall

_____ of the glory of God . . .

Romans 3:23

SIN SEPARATES YOU FROM GOD.

But your _____ have separated you from your _____ ;
your _____ have hidden his _____ from you . . .

Isaiah 59:2

No "good deeds", "good intentions", or "religious acts" (church attendance, being born of Christian parents, or rituals like baptism, communion, paying tithes, etc.) can take away our sins and get us to God.

```
                    works
        SINFUL   philosophy      HOLY
         MAN      religion        GOD
```

ETERNAL PUNISHMENT IS THE PENALTY FOR SIN.

For the _____ of sin is _____ .

Romans 6:23

If anyone's name (write your name here _____)
was not found written in the book of _____ , he was
thrown into the lake of _____ .

Revelation 20:15

Third base (Step 3) is so close to scoring. Here we understand that God sent His Son, Jesus Christ, to die on the cross in our place. Only by His sacrifice may we advance home.

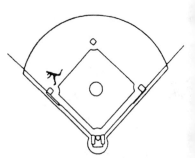

DEFINITIONS:

Righteous — "One who does what is right."

Urighteous — "One who does not do what is right."

GOD SENT HIS SON.

But God _____ His own love for us _____
(write your name here)
in this: While we were still _____ ,
Christ _____ for us.

Romans 5:8

CHRIST DIED IN OUR PLACE.

For _____ died for _____ once for all, the righteous for the _____ , to bring _____ to God.

1 Peter 3:18

JESUS IS THE ONLY WAY TO GOD.

Jesus answered "I am the _____ and the _____ and the _____ . No _____ comes to the _____ except through _____ .

John 14:6

The blood of Jesus pays for all your sins and satisfies God's righteous requirement for justice so that you may enter His presence! However, it is not enough just to stay on third base knowing these facts.

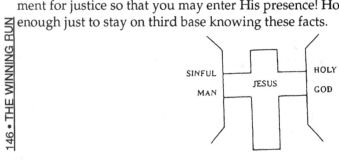

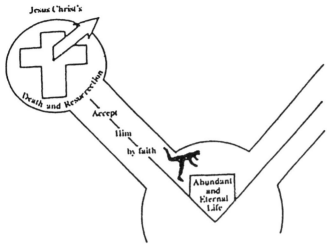

YOU MUST TRUST CHRIST.

_____ on the Lord Jesus
Christ and you will be _____ .

Acts 16:31

Yet to all who _____ Him, to those
who _____ in His name,
He gave the _____ to become
_____ of God.

John 1:12

DEFINITIONS:

Believe — "To take as true."
Receive — "To take into one's posession.
To accept."
Justified — "To free from blame."
Grace — "Unmerited favor."
Redemption — "To buy back, to set free."
Condemnation — "Proof of guilt."

HIS DEATH IS PAYMENT IN FULL FOR ALL YOUR SIN.

. . . justified _____ by His _____ through the
_____ that came by Christ Jesus.

Romans 3:24

Therefore, there is now no _____ for those who are
_____ Christ Jesus.

Romans 8:1

SALVATION IS BY GRACE AND NOT BY WORKS.

For it is by _____ you have been saved, through _____
— and this not from _____ , it is the _____ of
God — not by _____ , so that no one can boast.

Ephesians 2:8, 9

Why not receive Jesus Christ as your Savior and Lord right now?

1.   Admit your sin to God (confess).

2.   Be willing to leave your sin (repent).

3.   Believe Jesus Christ died for you on the cross (believe).

4.   Ask Jesus to forgive your sins, come into your heart, and take control of your life (receive).

HERE IS A SUGGESTED PRAYER:

Dear God,

    I know I am a sinner. I am sorry for my sins and want to leave them. I believe Jesus died for me and I now invite Him to come into my life and to make me what He wants me to be.

                Thank you

             _____
             (signed)

If you sincerely prayed this prayer, Christ came into your life as He promised. You scored the "Winning Run" by the grace of God! Don't just sit in the dugout. Remember to **study God's Word** (this book can help you get started), **tell others** how they can receive Jesus, **find fellowship** with others who know Jesus, and **pray regularly** for His guidance. **Obey** His teachings as proof of your love for Him!

Congratulations! You are now in a position to become strong in character!

THE PERFECT RELIEVER

THE FOLLOWING BASEBALL illustration explains how to walk consistently in the power of the Holy Spirit, our only hope for victory over the world, our own sinful nature, and the devil:

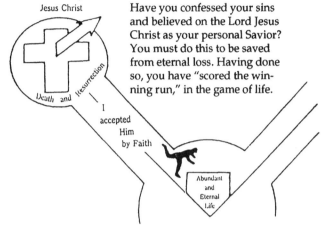

Jesus Christ

Death and Resurrection

I accepted Him by Faith

Abundant and Eternal Life

Have you confessed your sins and believed on the Lord Jesus Christ as your personal Savior? You must do this to be saved from eternal loss. Having done so, you have "scored the winning run," in the game of life.

WHO HAS LIFE?

He who has the _____ has _____ ; he who does not have the _____ of _____ does not have _____ .

1 John 5:12

YOU SIGNED WITH THE WINNING TEAM
WHEN YOU RECEIVED CHRIST!

1. For he has _____ us from the dominion of _____ and brought us into the _____ of the _____ he loves, in whom we have _____ , the _____ of sins.

Colossians 1:13, 14

2. Yet to all who _____ him, to those who _____ in his name, he gave the right to become _____ of God.

John 1:12

3. Having _____ , you were marked in him with a _____ , the promised _____ _____ , who is a deposit _____ , our inheritance until the _____ of those who are God's _____ — to the praise of his glory.

Ephesians 1:13, 14

BUT .... WHAT'S HAPPENING NOW?

Though our Lord has assured all His
children of eternal life (John 10:28) and our
position in Christ never changes, our practice
may sometimes bring dishonor to God.
The enemy rally makes life miserable.

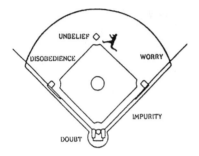

The enemy's dugout:
> Prayerlessness
> No desire for Bible Study
> Loss of love
> Legalistic attitude
> Jealousy
> Guilt

This rally must be stopped, for the Bible makes it clear that no one who be-
longs to God can continually practice sin (1 John 2:3; 3:6-10).

These two pitchers' mounds represent
the two lifestyles from which a Christian must choose:

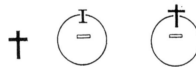

Self in control of the game and
Christ's Resurrection power
waiting in the bullpen — enemy rally produces discord.

For the _____ nature
desires what is _____
to the _____ .

Power of Christ replaces self on
the mound — rally is stopped
and peace is restored.

. . . and the _____ what is
_____ to the
_____ nature .
Galatians 5:17a

SO WHAT'S THE SOLUTION?

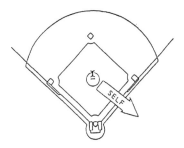

BRING IN THE PERFECT RELIEVER!

We must step off the mound and allow God to have complete authority by giving control of the game to the Holy Spirit.

Only by giving the Holy Spirit of God His rightful place of authority over our every thought, word and deed, can we consistently overcome defeat and despair.

Since we live by the _____, let us keep in _____ with the _____.

Galatians 5:25

WHAT DOES THE HOLY SPIRIT DO?

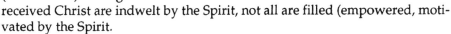

When you received Jesus Christ as Savior, the Holy Spirit indwelt you (Romans 8:9). Though all who have received Christ are indwelt by the Spirit, not all are filled (empowered, motivated by the Spirit.

The Holy Spirit:

1. Teaches us all things and reminds us of Jesus' words (John 14:26).   T   F
2. Brings glory to Jesus by guiding us into all truth (John 16:13-15).   T   F
3. Convicts us of sin (John 16:7-8).   T   F
4. Gives us power to talk of Jesus (Acts 1:8).   T   F
5. Assures us we belong to Jesus and enables us to live above circumstances via prayer (Romans 8:26).   T   F
6. Flows from us as the source of abundant victory (John 7:37-39).   T   F

HOW CAN YOU BE FILLED?

You can be filled (motivated) by
the Holy Spirit right now if you are
willing to step off the mound of
your life and give the ball to the
Master Coach.

You were taught, with regard to your _____ way of life, to put
_____ your _____ self, which is being _____ by
its _____ desires; to be made _____ in the attitude
of your _____ ; and to put _____ the _____ self, created
to be like _____ in true _____ and _____ .

Ephesians 4:22-24

The Master Coach will not replace you on the mound against your heart's
desire. Just as in receiving Christ, living consistently in His power is a matter
of your will.

The Keys to Victory

1. For we know that our old _____ was _____
   with him so that the body of _____ might be done
   away with, that we should no longer be _____ to
   _____ — because anyone who has _____ has
   been freed from _____ .

   Romans 6:6-7

2. In the same way, _____ yourselves _____ to _____
   but _____ to God in Christ Jesus.

   Romans 6:11

3. For sin shall not be your _____, because you are not under
   _____ , but under _____ .

   Romans 6:14

PRESENT YOURSELF TO GOD THROUGH PRAYER!

HOW DO YOU KNOW YOU ARE FILLED BY THE HOLY SPIRIT?

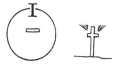

This is the_____ we have in approaching _____ : that if we ask _____ according to his _____ , he _____ us. And if we _____ that he _____ us — whatever we ask — we _____ that we _____ what we ask of him.

1 John 5:14-15

Is it God's will that you be filled (motivated) by His Spirit? He has said so (Ephesians 5:18). Therefore, based upon the authority of God's Word and His trustworthiness, you can KNOW you are filled with His Spirit regardless of your emotions.

WHAT IF SELF TRIES TO GET BACK INTO THE GAME?

The self life is a deadly enemy of the control of the Holy Spirit. Often self will try to return to the game, and when that happens, Satan quickly reloads the bases. If you sense this happening, take these steps:

1. Confess all known sin to God and thank Him. He has forgiven you (1 John 1:9).

2. Trust Christ to again fill you with the Holy Spirit, who will once more take control (Ephesians 5:18).

WHAT WILL GOD'S PERFECT RELIEVER ACCOMPLISH IN YOUR LIFE?

He will retire all doubt, fear, worry and other sins that run the bases of your life. He will substitute love, joy, peace and other fruits.

> But the fruit of the Spirit is love, joy, peace, patience, kindness, goodness, faithfulness, gentleness and self-control. Against such things there is no law.
>
> Galatians 5:22-23

His assortment of pitches includes truth, faith, righteousness and other weapons through which daily victory is assured.

> Finally, be strong in the Lord and in his mighty power. Put on the full armor of God so that you can take your stand against the devil's schemes. For our struggle is not against flesh and blood, but against the rulers, against the authorities, against the powers of this dark world and against the spiritual forces of evil in the heavenly realms. Therefore put on the full armor of God, so that when the day of evil comes, you may be able to stand your ground, and after you have done everything, to stand. Stand firm then, with the belt of truth buckled around your waist, with the breastplate of righteousness in place, and with your feet fitted with the readiness that comes from the gospel of peace. In addition to all this, take up the shield of faith, with which you can extinguish all the flaming arrows of the evil one. Take the helmet of salvation and the sword of the Spirit, which is the word of God. And pray in the Spirit on all occasions with all kinds of prayers and requests. With this in mind, be alert and always keep on praying for all saints.
>
> Ephesians 6:10-18

He will turn your eyes to the Master Coach, Jesus Christ, and conform you to His likeness.

> And we, who with unveiled faces all reflect the Lord's glory, are being transformed into his likeness with ever-increasing glory, which comes from the Lord, who is Spirit.
>
> 2 Corinthians 3:18

You can praise and thank God through trials and suffering in the game of life, knowing He has a plan for you.

> Consider it pure joy, my brothers, whenever you face trials of many kinds, because you know that the testing of your faith develops perseverance.
>
> James 1:2-3

The final score will bring much glory to God!